Online Student Skills and Strategies Handbook

Loyd R. Ganey Jr., Ph.D.
Western International University

Frank L. Christ
*Emeritus, California State University
Long Beach
Visiting Scholar University of Texas at Austin*

Victor R. Hurt
*Department of Defense–Fort Huachuca,
Arizona*

PEARSON
Longman

New York San Francisco Boston
London Toronto Sydney Tokyo Singapore Madrid
Mexico City Munich Paris Cape Town Hong Kong Montreal

Senior Acquisitions Editor: Susan Kunchandy
Senior Marketing Manager: Melanie Craig
Supplements Editor: Donna Campion
Production Manager: Stacey Kulig
Project Coordination, Text Design, and Electronic Page Makeup: Electronic Publishing Services
    Inc., NYC
Cover Design Manager: Wendy Ann Fredericks
Cover Designer: Joe DePinho
Cover Illustration/Photo: © Corbis Royalty Free
Senior Manufacturing Buyer: Al Dorsey
Printer and Binder: R.R. Donnelley Crawfordsville
Cover Printer: Phoenix Color Corporation

Credits/acknowledgments:
Adobe product screen shots reprinted with permission from Adobe Systems Incorporated.
Google web site screen shots reprinted with permission from Google Incorporated.
Microsoft product screen shots reprinted with permission from Microsoft Incorporated.
Netscape and the "N" Logo are registered trademarks of Netscape Communications Corporation.
Netscape content © 2005 Netscape Communications Corporation. Used with permission.

Library of Congress Cataloging-in-Publication Data

Ganey, Loyd R.
  Online student skills and strategies handbook / Loyd R. Ganey, Frank L. Christ, Victor R. Hurt.
    p. cm.
  Includes bibliographical references and index.
  ISBN 0-321-31684-3 (paperbound)
  1. Computer-assisted instruction—United States—Handbooks, manuals, etc. 2. Internet in
higher education—United States—Handbooks, manuals, etc. I. Christ, Frank L. II. Hurt, Victor R.
III. Title.
LB1028.5.G355 2006
371.33'4--dc22
                        2005012946

Please visit our website at http://www.ablongman.com

ISBN 0-321-31684-3

1 2 3 4 5 6 7 8 9 10—DOC—08 07 06 05

Contents

iv   Contents

CHAPTER 3   Online Email Tasks for Online Learning   84

CHAPTER 4   Online Course Tasks for Online Learning   131

CHAPTER 5   Online Student/Learner Tasks for Online Learning   151

CHAPTER 6   Online Learning Pitfall Solutions   168

About the Authors

Loyd Ganey

Loyd R. Ganey Jr. has been instructing students for over 25 years and for the past 10 years greatly involved in distance education as a student, developer, and instructor. A retired U.S. Army chaplain, he is currently a professor of behavioral sciences for Western International University and works as an instructor, developer, and consultant for several academic institutions. Ganey is involved in committees and organizations that specialize in distance education and conducts presentations at the local, state, and national levels on distance education. He has a professional certificate in instructional design for online learning from Capella University and has developed over 30 online courses using Web Course in a Box, WebBoard, WebCT, eCollege, and BlackBoard. He completed his Ph.D. (2000) in human services from Capella University. In 1988 he received a Master of Science in professional counseling from Georgia State University and completed six quarters of clinical pastoral education. He obtained a Master of Divinity (1980) from Abilene Christian University, and a B.A. in humanities interdisciplinary studies and a B.A. in religious studies in 1977 from the University of West Florida. Ganey enjoys working with online students and ensuring their survival and success in the online environment.

Frank Christ

Frank L. Christ has been involved with learning support for students, faculty, and corporate managers for the past 30 years. He is the founder and director (1972–1999) of the award-winning Learning Assistance Support System at California State University, Long Beach. In addition, he is a visiting scholar for the University Learning Center, University of Arizona, and for the Learning Center at the University of Texas at Austin, where he currently co-directs the Winter Institute for Learning Support Center administrators and staff. Christ has been teaching online graduate courses at Grambling State University for the past five years. His publications, workshops, and consulting focus on academic support for online students and integrating student learning and study strategies into online courses. He is the co-developer and content editor for the web portal Learning Support Centers in Higher Education, which can be viewed at http://www.pvc.maricopa.edu/~lsche.

Victor R. Hurt has been working in the computer and Internet field for more than 10 years and has built numerous personal, commercial, and government websites. He has spent the last six years working as the webmaster for a Department of Defense organization overseeing the development, maintenance, and continual growth of five corporate-level websites. Hurt has a Bachelor of Science degree in information systems from Western International University. He has also taken numerous courses in web

Victor Hurt

design, management, and security. He has designed and engineered numerous local area networks (LANs) supporting from 10 to 200 users and has also been a system administrator for several private and public organizations.

Introduction to Online Instructors

Our purpose in authoring this handbook with a companion website is to give online instructors a tool to help their students develop and improve the skills and competencies that are necessary for success in online courses. We designed the *Online Student Skills and Strategies Handbook* as a series of step-by-step tutorials that can be used by students at the time an online course question or problem arises. We envision this handbook open and lying flat in front of a student's computer screen for just-in-time use as needed. We also see this handbook functioning as a 24/7 aid to instructors, since they can recommend specific tutorials when students need specific help with a course assignment or course task. We believe that more students can be retained and achieve greater course success if such academic support for student learning is immediately available. We also believe that this support should be specific to student problems in online course tasks and assignments.

We regard online study and learning as somewhat different from traditional classroom learning, although we agree that much of the learning and study strategies recommended to students in current how-to-study texts and on institutional web pages can be useful to online students. However, based on our experience with online students, we believe their online learning assignments require learning, communications, and technological competencies specifically focused on the tasks and assignments required of them in online courses.

We have found no text or online collection of material that was immediately accessible and easily usable by online students as they encounter course-related questions or problems. And as most online instructors know, students do have problems—problems in readiness for online learning, problems with computer competencies and course assignments, learning and study skills problems relevant to online learning, and even basic skills proficiency problems.

Most current texts that purport to assist online students with learning and study problems are descriptive and hortative; seldom are they instructional and tutorial. Although the web offers many pages of learning and study assistance for online students, much of this assistance is transitory, with web pages being discontinued or restricted to matriculated students at an institution. The *Online Student Skills and Strategies Handbook* is designed to be accessible and useful whenever an online student needs assistance. It exemplifies the current "just in time" training philosophy since, as a printed handbook sitting next to a student's computer, it will allow a student to quickly look up information and learn or review skills and course procedures at the moment they are needed.

In addition, the *Online Student Skills and Strategies Handbook* can be useful as a text for orientation programs. It contains both student self-report surveys and prescriptions for students to follow as they note their online problems and concerns.

From our experience in reviewing the current literature on online teaching and learning, we have found that the literature emphasizes teaching rather than student learning. We have found that institutions and organizations that offered online courses and degrees freely used the terms "student support" and "student resources" on their websites. We also found that although most institutions had a section on student resources, it tended to focus on Internet research. Not many institutions and organizations deliver academic support for online students. There is a lot of material in print and on the Internet that speaks to student online readiness. However, it is rare to find institutional web pages that focus on student learning and study strategies and competencies that are specifically designed to assist students with the course tasks and assignments that are required for online course success.

The use of the terms "learning" and "student/learner support" in many distance education articles initially gave us hope that we would find more than hortatory advice to students about their learning skills. What we found is a disparity between the titles of articles and presentations that use the term "online learning" and their content, in which we did not find any reference to learning or study strategies. The emphasis seemed to be on Internet skills rather than on learning/study skills. As we did searches on Internet search engines like Google, Alta Vista, and Yahoo using the phrase "learning support for online students," we found minimal results that would be useful for online students or that could be recommended by online instructors when their students experienced difficulties with their online course assignments. This is not to say that the Internet does not contain a wealth of helpful tutorial material, especially in the areas of computer literacy and learning and study strategies. However, to access and use these web tutorials, students must leave their courseware screens in order that they can view the tutorials. We believe it is preferable for students simply to look up their immediate problem, turn to a relevant tutorial in the handbook, and step through directions to solve their problems.

Following this introduction and a subsequent introduction to students, Chapter 1 of the *Online Student Skills and Strategies Handbook* provides five readiness assessments keyed to prescriptive tutorials located in the chapters listed below:

- **Chapter 2.** Computer Tasks for Online Learning
- **Chapter 3.** Online Email Tasks for Online Learning
- **Chapter 4.** Online Course Tasks for Online Learning
- **Chapter 5.** Online Student/Learner Tasks for Online Learning
- **Chapter 6.** Online Learning Pitfall Solutions

Each step-by-step tutorial follows a six-part format:

- Title
- Introduction
- Online Use of the Competency/Skill
- Step-by-Step Directions to develop or improve the competency/skill
- Internet Resources for the competency/skill
- Other Relevant Tutorials in the text

A Webliography, Computer Skills Performance Tips, a Glossary, and an Index conclude the handbook.

As part of our author responsibility, we will maintain web pages on the publisher's site to update both web and text references to online learning and study assistance.

Also available for students is Longman's Student Planner (0-321-04573-4).

We hope that you might consider including this handbook in your course syllabi and refer to it in your course announcements. You might also require it as one of the texts for your course, as an ancillary text, or to suggest it as "recommended, but not required." If you use the text, you might want to give a quiz on its contents in the first or second week of the course. In addition, you might want to embed references to specific skills and competencies in your email or course announcements, lectures, and assignments, citing specific pages where the tutorials are located.

Our intent in writing this handbook is to give you a set of tutorials that your students can use not only in preparation for course activities, but also as just-in-time assistance whenever students need help in completing a course activity or assignment. We strongly encourage you to point your students to the help desk or help manual that your specific courseware management system (CMS) provides. Some courseware providers offer some very thorough help manuals, and one of the early tasks of any online student or online faculty is to learn how to navigate and use the courseware.

The *Online Student Skills and Strategies Handbook* will greatly assist online faculty in focusing on subject matter content rather than assisting students with computer and technology skills, courseware skills, and study skills and strategies.

Acknowledgments

Loyd Ganey, Frank Christ, and Victor Hurt would like to thank the following colleagues and friends.

Loyd Ganey is grateful for his parents, Loyd and Dorothy Ganey, who instilled within him the adventurous spirit of lifelong learning. He is thankful for his wife, Gerlinde, who seemingly never tires of listening to his passion for distance education. Many thanks go out to the hundreds of online students who gave him inspiration and encouragement for this project.

Frank Christ gives thanks to Alice Christ, his wife of many decades, for her encouragement and sometime manuscript proofreading, to his Number 3 son, Michael P. Christ, a technical writer/editor, who gave great editorial advice, and to all of his Grambling State University online graduate students who inspired him to articulate tutorial solutions to their course problems.

Victor Hurt would like to thank his wife, Sherry, for her patience and encouragement not only for this undertaking, but also for all of his varied endeavors.

The authors are thankful to Susan Kunchandy and her very talented and friendly staff at Pearson/Longman for their insights, guidance, editing, and encouragement.

We would appreciate receiving your feedback or comments regarding the *Online Student Skills and Strategies Handbook*. Please email us at: drganey@ cox.net or flchris@cox.net.

We wish to acknowledge the contributions of reviewers, who have provided valuable suggestions in the development of this text:

Gwyn Enright, San Diego City College
Diana Nystedt, Palo Alto College
Michael Palagonia, Chandler-Gilbert Community College
Pamela K. S. Patrick, Capella University
Maria Sortino, Sortino International Training
Teresa Tatum, Capella University
Rick Sheets, Paradise Valley Community College
Jennifer K. Pauken, Heartland Community College

Introduction to Online Students

You, the online student, are the vital and essential part of a very exciting time in the merger of technology and education—the dynamic growth of online education. Today, online education offers computer-based instructional environments that expand learning opportunities and can provide top-quality education while meeting the special needs of adult learners who want to continue their education. Online education offers a convenient and flexible solution to pursue your academic and career goals while juggling the multiple demands of family, work, and other schedule requirements. Colleges and universities have found that online programs are essential in providing access to education for working adults, lifelong learners, people with physical disabilities, parents with young children, and geographically displaced students. For any online program to be successful, the curriculum, the instructor, the technology, and you, the online student, must be carefully considered in order to realize the full advantage of the strengths of this unique, challenging, and exciting way of learning.

Overview of the *Online Student Skills and Strategies Handbook*

The concept of the *Online Student Skills and Strategies Handbook* came out of instructing hundreds of online students and seeing semester after semester that online students require unique skills and competencies to survive and succeed. The authors combined years of online course development, distance education consulting and presentations, online course instruction, and the experience of being online students themselves, and came to the necessary conclusion that online students are in great need of specific tutorials which will make their online education a successful and enjoyable learning experience. In fact, online students have requested many of the tutorials in this book.

Being an online learner requires some unique and specific skills and competencies that are quite different from those necessary for success in traditional face-to face (F2F) courses. The *Online Student Skills and Strategies Handbook* focuses on specific and practical step-by-step tutorials, which will greatly enhance your online learning experience.

Chapter 1, the introductory chapter in this handbook, lets you look at yourself to determine if you are ready to be successful in online courses. It contains five questionnaires. Each questionnaire is keyed to one of the subsequent handbook chapters and its specific tutorials that you can complete. As you will see, the questionnaires go beyond these personal assessments of your attitude, motivation, and technological and learning readiness by pointing you to specific tutorials in the subsequent five chapters of this handbook to develop or strengthen areas that may cause problems in your online coursework.

As you complete the questionnaires, reflect on your needs and concerns. Answer all questions honestly. There are no scores. Your answers will indicate your strengths and potential problems. They will also point you to specific step-by-step tutorials in this handbook to help you be a successful online student.

Chapter 2, Computer Tasks for Online Learning, focuses on the importance of essential computer tasks that are critical for your success as an online student. This chapter covers configuring and organizing your computer to do basic computer tasks.

Chapter 3, Online Email Tasks for Online Learning, focuses on specific email skills and functions that will enable and empower your online learning experience.

Chapter 4, Online Course Tasks for Online Learning, focuses on skills, competencies, and resources within your online course. The tutorials help you use specific courseware tools to make your online learning experience pleasurable and successful.

Chapter 5, Online Student/Learner Tasks for Online Learning, looks at learning tasks that you will be doing as you begin, work through, and complete your online courses.

Chapter 6, Online Learning Pitfall Solutions, considers personal problem areas that you may encounter as an online student and points you toward solutions.

As you encounter a course activity or assignment problem, you can turn to the Index in this handbook, where you will find the page references to a tutorial that takes you step-by-step through simple directions to complete the task. Keep this handbook on your desk so you can solve any of the problems that come up as you move through your online course.

The Demands of Online Learning

The *Online Student Skills and Strategies Handbook* provides very practical step-by-step tutorials that speak to the demands of your online learning. Online courses can be more demanding than traditional classroom courses. You may have found out already that many students have an immediate learning curve in online learning. To be a successful online student, you do need some degree of computer literacy and some specific online computer skills. The step-by-step tutorials in Chapter 2 will be a great asset to you in meeting the additional computer demands of being an online student.

One of the more critical computer skills that will truly enhance your online learning experiences is using email efficiently and effectively. Chapter 3 offers a range of tutorials to strengthen your email skills.

A significant learning curve for you as an online student is familiarization with the online course environment. This includes specific course tasks and the various tools within the online course that are invaluable assets and resources for you. Chapter 4 provides the step-by-step tutorials that will help you to navigate and master your online course environment. These tutorials will help you become very familiar with how your online course functions and the unique demands of the online learning environment.

Many colleges and universities have learning centers and provide students with guidance and instruction in learning skills applicable to face-to-face courses, but not to the unique and challenging environment of online learning. Many academic institutions are beginning to realize this void and the necessity of speaking to specific online student skills. Chapter 5 looks at some specific online tasks that will strengthen your ability to survive and succeed in online courses. These step-by-step tutorials will give you some very practical skills to enable you to meet the demands of online learning.

Learning at a distance requires an additional degree of perseverance and self-direction. You need to manage your time efficiently, take the initiative to keep up with your class work, and be diligent to meet assignment deadlines. As an online student, you will find that the online learning process is normally accelerated and requires great commitment on your part. Keeping up with the class and completing all work on time is vital. Once you get behind, it is almost impossible to catch up. Basically, you need to maintain your motivation as an online student; you must really want to thrive and learn in the online environment. Chapter 6 offers step-by-step tutorials to overcome or prevent certain personal problems that arise in the demands of online learning.

Readiness for Online Learning

If this is your first online course, hopefully you have already taken a readiness assessment for online or distance education that your institution offered. You may also have completed an orientation for new online students or a special orientation to the courseware (Blackboard, WebCT, eCollege, and others) that you will be using. Many students have marched into distance education thinking that it is going to be a cakewalk, a smooth glide, and easy pickings. Alas, the attrition rates as a whole are higher in online courses than in traditional face-to-face courses. So it is best to ensure that you have the basic skills and readiness factors to assure your success in the online environment. You need to be ready not only to survive, but also to succeed.

Some Final Thoughts

The online learning environment is on the cutting edge of learning today. The meld of education and technology has dramatically transformed distance education. Originally, distance education referred to correspondence courses and communicating with instructors using the postal service and telephone. However, it now centers on the use of computers and Internet technologies. New technologies have removed many obstacles and provided benefits for everyone involved. The use of technology has also created new kinds of challenges for students in distance education.

The *Online Student Skills and Strategies Handbook* is a book that has been developed out of the frustrations and problems that online students have expressed to the authors. You have spoken. We have listened. This handbook will give you the practical skills to meet the challenges of online education and prepare you for a successful and rewarding online learning experience.

CHAPTER 1

Readiness
for Online Learning

Introduction

This chapter contains five self-assessments that will help you to assess your knowledge and skills for online courses and their assignments. Please take the time to answer these self-assessments that measure your online course readiness and competencies. If you know the information and if you have the skills mentioned in these self-assessments, you will be a successful and satisfied online student. Most of these assessments are self-report questionnaires and require your honest reflection and answers to gain meaningful results. These self-assessments will help to determine if you are ready for online learning in the key areas of technical literacy, Internet literacy, awareness and understanding of online education, and online student skills.

Online Use of the Competency/Skill

In this chapter, you will find out if you have the technical and student learning skills necessary to succeed with online learning as you complete the following five self-assessments:

Your Readiness for Online Computer Tasks (Chapter 2 Self-Assessment)

Your Readiness for Online Email Tasks (Chapter 3 Self-Assessment)

Your Readiness for Online Course Tasks (Chapter 4 Self-Assessment)

Your Readiness for Online Learning Tasks (Chapter 5 Self-Assessment)

Your Readiness for Online Learning Pitfall Solutions (Chapter 6 Self-Assessment)

These self-assessments are in the form of yes/no questionnaires. You are acquiring insight into your skills and abilities as these relate to preparation for online learning. Remember: the online learning environment is quite different from the traditional classroom environment.

Answer honestly for the most meaningful results. All "No" or "Unknown" answers will lead you to specific information and/or a tutorial that will assist you in being successful in your online learning courses.

Chapter 2 Assessment: Computer Tasks for Online Learning

Self-Report Assessment—Online Learning Computer Tasks

Please assess your computer skills and knowledge for the following:

1. I know the minimum hardware/software configuration required by my Online Campus.
    If no or unknown, please refer to 2.1
    ☐ Yes   ☐ No   ☐ Unknown

2. I know how to enable cookies.
    If no or unknown, please refer to 2.2
    ☐ Yes   ☐ No   ☐ Unknown

3. I know how to enable JavaScript.
    If no or unknown, please refer to 2.3
    ☐ Yes   ☐ No   ☐ Unknown

4. I know how to access web pages.
    If no or unknown, please refer to 2.4
    ☐ Yes   ☐ No   ☐ Unknown

5. I know how to bookmark websites and pages.
    If no or unknown, please refer to 2.5
    ☐ Yes   ☐ No   ☐ Unknown

6. I know how to add necessary plug-ins (i.e. Acrobat Reader, Real Audio, etc.) to my computer.
    If no or unknown, please refer to 2.6
    ☐ Yes   ☐ No   ☐ Unknown

7. I know how to clear my cache.
    If no or unknown, please refer to 2.7
    ☐ Yes   ☐ No   ☐ Unknown

8. I know how to set my computer monitor resolution for best viewing.
    If no or unknown, please refer to 2.8
    ☐ Yes   ☐ No   ☐ Unknown

9. I know how to set my zoom control for document viewing.
    If no or unknown, please refer to 2.9
    ☐ Yes   ☐ No   ☐ Unknown

10. I know how to create and organize files and folders.
    If no or unknown, please refer to 2.10
    ☐ Yes   ☐ No   ☐ Unknown

11. I know how to copy and paste.
    If no or unknown, please refer to 2.11
    ☐ Yes   ☐ No   ☐ Unknown

12. I know how to copy and paste Internet addresses from my screen.
    If no or unknown, please refer to 2.12
    ☐ Yes   ☐ No   ☐ Unknown

13. I know how to copy and paste from a pdf file (Acrobat Reader).
☐ Yes ☐ No ☐ Unknown
If no or unknown, please refer to 2.13

14. I know how to save a file.
☐ Yes ☐ No ☐ Unknown
If no or unknown, please refer to 2.14

15. I know how to upload a file.
☐ Yes ☐ No ☐ Unknown
If no or unknown, please refer to 2.15

16. I know how to convert files to rich text format.
☐ Yes ☐ No ☐ Unknown
If no or unknown, please refer to 2.16

17. I know how to open and use two or more screens in Windows.
☐ Yes ☐ No ☐ Unknown
If no or unknown, please refer to 2.17

18. I know how to protect my computer from viruses.
☐ Yes ☐ No ☐ Unknown
If no or unknown, please refer to 2.18

19. I know how to set security measures for my computer.
☐ Yes ☐ No ☐ Unknown
If no or unknown, please refer to 2.19

Chapter 3 Assessment: Email Tasks for Online Learning

Self-Report Assessment—Online Learning Email Tasks

Please assess your computer skills and knowledge for the following:

1. I know how to effectively use email in my online courses.
☐ Yes ☐ No ☐ Unknown
If no or unknown, please refer to 3.1

2. I know how to access email.
☐ Yes ☐ No ☐ Unknown
If no or unknown, please refer to 3.2

3. I know how to ensure my emails correctly identify me as the sender.
☐ Yes ☐ No ☐ Unknown
If no or unknown, please refer to 3.3

4. I know how to add an email signature to my emails.
☐ Yes ☐ No ☐ Unknown
If no or unknown, please refer to 3.4

5. I know how to effectively proofread my email.
☐ Yes ☐ No ☐ Unknown
If no or unknown, please refer to 3.5

6. I know the basic standards of email   ☐ Yes   ☐ No   ☐ Unknown
   etiquette.
   If no or unknown, please refer to 3.6

7. I know how to save email to folders.   ☐ Yes   ☐ No   ☐ Unknown
   If no or unknown, please refer to 3.7

8. I know how to attach files to emails.   ☐ Yes   ☐ No   ☐ Unknown
   If no or unknown, please refer to 3.8

9. I know how to protect my computer   ☐ Yes   ☐ No   ☐ Unknown
   from email viruses.
   If no or unknown, please refer to 3.9

10. I know how to save my email to draft   ☐ Yes   ☐ No   ☐ Unknown
    mode so I can think about it before
    I send.
    If no or unknown, please refer to 3.10

11. I know how to set a high priority on   ☐ Yes   ☐ No   ☐ Unknown
    my emails.
    If no or unknown, please refer to 3.11

12. I know how to clean and maintain   ☐ Yes   ☐ No   ☐ Unknown
    my email account by periodically
    emptying the trash and sent folders.
    If no or unknown, please refer to 3.12

Chapter 4 Assessment: Online Course Tasks for Online Learning
Self-Report Assessment—Online Learning Course Tasks

Please assess your Online Learning skills and knowledge for the following:

1. I know how to access my course
   anytime, anywhere—even from   ☐ Yes   ☐ No   ☐ Unknown
   another computer.
   If no or unknown, please refer to 4.1

2. I know how to save and access all my   ☐ Yes   ☐ No   ☐ Unknown
   pertinent course information: college
   and course web address (URL),
   username, and password.
   If no or unknown, please refer to 4.2

3. I know how to navigate my entire   ☐ Yes   ☐ No   ☐ Unknown
   online course and what information
   all tabs and buttons contain.
   If no or unknown, please refer to 4.3

4. I know how to find and overview all   ☐ Yes   ☐ No   ☐ Unknown
   important online course materials:

syllabus, assignments, grading
policy, and other important course
information.

If no or unknown, please refer to 4.4

5. I know how to print out all important   ☐ Yes   ☐ No   ☐ Unknown
online course materials.

If no or unknown, please refer to 4.5

6. I know how to utilize the course   ☐ Yes   ☐ No   ☐ Unknown
syllabus and know how it ties into all
aspects of the online course.

If no or unknown, please refer to 4.6

7. I know how to participate in discussion   ☐ Yes   ☐ No   ☐ Unknown
boards.

If no or unknown, please refer to 4.7

8. I know the importance of using   ☐ Yes   ☐ No   ☐ Unknown
appropriate netiquette in discussion
boards.

If no or unknown, please refer to 4.8

9. I know how to create a new thread or   ☐ Yes   ☐ No   ☐ Unknown
discussion in the online course
discussion board.

If no or unknown, please refer to 4.9

10. I know how to reply correctly in a   ☐ Yes   ☐ No   ☐ Unknown
discussion board to my instructor
and/or fellow students.

If no or unknown, please refer to 4.10

11. I know how to submit my assignments   ☐ Yes   ☐ No   ☐ Unknown
within the online course or via email.

If no or unknown, please refer to 4.11

12. I know how to access and participate   ☐ Yes   ☐ No   ☐ Unknown
in a live chat.

If no or unknown, please refer to 4.12

13. I know how to communicate effectively   ☐ Yes   ☐ No   ☐ Unknown
within a live chat.

If no or unknown, please refer to 4.13

14. I know how to access and utilize   ☐ Yes   ☐ No   ☐ Unknown
special tools within my online course
(gradebook, personal profile, calendar,
external weblinks, etc.).

If no or unknown, please refer to 4.14

15. I know how to locate and open the   ☐ Yes   ☐ No   ☐ Unknown
courseware help or student help
manual from my online course.
If no or unknown, please refer to 4.15

Chapter 5 Assessment: Online Student/Learner Tasks for Online Learning

Self-Report Assessment—Online Student/Learner Tasks

Please assess your online learning skills and knowledge for the following:

1. I know how to create a course binder   ☐ Yes   ☐ No   ☐ Unknown
for offline reading and studying
If no or unknown, please refer to 5.1

2. I know how to effectively overview   ☐ Yes   ☐ No   ☐ Unknown
computer screen documents.
If no or unknown, please refer to 5.2

3. I use a method to take notes on what   ☐ Yes   ☐ No   ☐ Unknown
I see on the screen.
If no or unknown, please refer to 5.3

4. I know how to function as a member   ☐ Yes   ☐ No   ☐ Unknown
of a group doing online group
assignments.
If no or unknown, please refer to 5.4

5. I use a method to complete my online   ☐ Yes   ☐ No   ☐ Unknown
course assignments successfully
and on time.
If no or unknown, please refer to 5.5

6. I know what plagiarism is, the   ☐ Yes   ☐ No   ☐ Unknown
consequences for it, and how I can
avoid it.
If no or unknown, please refer to 5.6

7. I can use appropriate bibliographic   ☐ Yes   ☐ No   ☐ Unknown
formats like APA or MLA if my course
instructor requires one.
If no or unknown, please refer to 5.7

8. I use a method to edit and proofread   ☐ Yes   ☐ No   ☐ Unknown
course writing assignments before
emailing or posting them.
If no or unknown, please refer to 5.8

9. I use a method to write my responses ☐ Yes ☐ No ☐ Unknown
   to assigned questions on course reading.
   If no or unknown, please refer to 5.9

10. I know how to write an annotated ☐ Yes ☐ No ☐ Unknown
    bibliography.
    If no or unknown, please refer to 5.10

11. I know how to write a research paper ☐ Yes ☐ No ☐ Unknown
    If no or unknown, please refer to 5.11

12. I use a method to prepare for and take ☐ Yes ☐ No ☐ Unknown
    tests and exams.
    If no or unknown, please refer to 5.12

Chapter 6 Assessment: Online Learning Pitfall Solutions

Self-Report Assessment—Online Learning Pitfall Solutions

Please assess your online learning skills and knowledge for the following:

1. I know how to cope with visual or ☐ Yes ☐ No ☐ Unknown
   physical stress while working on my
   computer.
   If no or unknown, please refer to 6.1

2. I know how to minimize eye strain. ☐ Yes ☐ No ☐ Unknown
   If no or unknown, please refer to 6.2

3. I know where to get help with any ☐ Yes ☐ No ☐ Unknown
   computer hardware or software
   problems that may occur.
   If no or unknown, please refer to 6.3

4. I know where to get help with Internet ☐ Yes ☐ No ☐ Unknown
   research.
   If no or unknown, please refer to 6.4

5. I know where to get help with problems ☐ Yes ☐ No ☐ Unknown
   that occur in my online course.
   If no or unknown, please refer to 6.5

6. I use a method to organize my course ☐ Yes ☐ No ☐ Unknown
   tasks and assignments.
   If no or unknown, please refer to 6.6

7. I have made my home online learning ☐ Yes ☐ No ☐ Unknown
   environment efficient and effective.
   If no or unknown, please refer to 6.7

8. I have a time management process
   that I follow that is compatible with
   my online course assignments.   ☐ Yes   ☐ No   ☐ Unknown

   If no or unknown, please refer to 6.8

9. I know where I can get discipline   ☐ Yes   ☐ No   ☐ Unknown
   specific tutorial help for any problem
   or question that I may have regarding
   course content.

   If no or unknown, please refer to 6.9

10. I know how to interact appropriately   ☐ Yes   ☐ No   ☐ Unknown
    with my course instructor.

    If no or unknown, please refer to 6.10

11. I know how to interact appropriately   ☐ Yes   ☐ No   ☐ Unknown
    with my fellow students.

    If no or unknown, please refer to 6.11

12. I know where to get help with study   ☐ Yes   ☐ No   ☐ Unknown
    strategies.

    If no or unknown, please refer to 6.12

13. I know where to get help with any   ☐ Yes   ☐ No   ☐ Unknown
    problems that I may have with basic
    reading, writing, and math skills.

    If no or unknown, please refer to 6.13

14. I know where to get specialized help   ☐ Yes   ☐ No   ☐ Unknown
    with any personal problems that may
    affect the success of my online course
    work.

    If no or unknown, please refer to 6.14

15. I know where to find and how to follow   ☐ Yes   ☐ No   ☐ Unknown
    directions for course assignments.

    If no or unknown, please refer to 6.15

CHAPTER 2
Computer Tasks for Online Learning

Introduction

Chapter 2 focuses on essential computer tasks that are critical for success as an online student: configuring and organizing your computer for online learning and for doing basic computer tasks. Even though this chapter is heavy on computer technology, the good news is you do not have to be a high-wired computer geek to succeed as an online student. You can succeed as an online student with the basic computer skills and competencies that are identified with the step-by-step tutorials of this chapter.

If you are going to delve into the online education environment, it is necessary for you to understand and develop your basic computer skills and competencies. Mastery of these skills that enhance your ability to accomplish projects and assignments with a computer is known as *computer literacy*. Basic computer skills include proficiency in such things as word processing, spreadsheet programs, online library research, email, chat, and Internet research. An online course requires you to integrate and apply computer knowledge and skills for required assignments.

This chapter takes you through step-by-step tutorials on configuring and organizing your computer and doing basic computer tasks. As you complete this chapter, you develop skills to help you succeed in the online learning environment.

2.1   Meeting Minimum Requirements for Your PC

Introduction

Money is usually the weightiest factor that determines "how much" personal computer (PC) someone buys. The saying "you get what you pay for" often holds true with computers. If possible, try to purchase a system that is above the bare minimum as far as such things as processor speed, the amount of random access memory (RAM), and hard drive size. It seems that operating system and application software grows considerably with each new version. As you install more software and use up hard drive space with programs and data, PCs tend to get slower. Although a "fast" machine will eventually get slower, you should be able to get several years' use out of it. A "slow" machine will only get slower, so you will soon be living with much frustration and looking to replace it.

While we do not endorse any particular company that makes or sells PCs, brand name PCs are often reliable and have good support in the event of problems. Many independent suppliers also have excellent products and outstanding support. If you are considering a "generic" system from an online dealer or an independent local dealer, try to get an idea of their reputation. A local dealer can often provide a quality product along with fast support that is close to you.

Online Use of the Competency/Skill

You will know some of the specifications, options, and accessories to look for or consider when shopping for a personal computer.

Recommended Requirements

- Processor speed: Pentium III 850 MHz, 256MB RAM, or better
- System: MS Windows 2000 SP2, XP SP1 (or MAC equivalent)
- Hard Drive: 20 GB
- CD/CDRW/DVD drive
- USB ports (for use with external Flash Drive and other peripherals)
- Modem: cable modem or DSL (150 Kbps)
- Monitor: 1024x768, 256 color
- Sound/Speakers: 8 bit soundcard, speakers, and headphones
- Browser: Internet Explorer 6.0 or Netscape 7.0 or later with appropriate plug-ins. Must have an Internet Service Provider (ISP).

INTERNET RESOURCES

University of Toledo Distance & eLearning, "Minimum Computer Requirements"
http://www.dl.utoledo.edu/minimum_require.htm

Florida Atlantic University, "Minimum Computer Requirements"
http://www.itss.fau.edu/computer.htm

Southwest Missouri State University, "Minimum Computer Requirements"
http://www.smsuonline.smsu.edu/getready/mincompreqs.htm

OTHER RELEVANT TUTORIALS

Chapter 2.6: Adding Plug-ins
Chapter 2.18: Protecting Your Computer from Viruses
Chapter 2.19: Setting Security Measures for Your Computer
Chapter 4.1: Accessing Your Course Anytime, Anywhere
Chapter 6.3: Getting Help with Computer Problems

2.2 Enabling Cookies

Introduction

An Internet Cookie is a small text string of data that a web server can store on your computer's hard drive to save information and help identify you to websites. Websites use cookies for a variety of reasons. They allow websites to implement shopping carts or to save your preferences so the website is "customized" with your preferred colors, content, and other options. Cookies do not store personally identifiable information. They use some unique identifier, like a number or number/letter combination. You can control how your browser handles cookies. You can allow all cookies, have your browser prompt you every time a website attempts to store a cookie, or choose some option in between.

Online Use of the Competency/Skill

You will understand the use of cookies and how to control the way they are handled by your web browser.

Step-by-Step Directions for Internet Explorer (IE)

Step 1. Go to the "Menu Bar," click on "Tools," and choose "Internet Options" (Figure 2.2.1).

Step 2. Click on the "Privacy" tab (Figure 2.2.2).

Step 3. Click on the "Advanced" button (Figure 2.2.2).

Step 4. Check the "Override automatic cookie handling" dialog box (Figure 2.2.3).

Step 5. Choose the options you prefer by clicking on the appropriate radio buttons (Figure 2.2.3).

Step 6. Click the "OK" button to close the Advanced Privacy Settings dialog box (Figure 2.2.3).

Step 7. Click the "OK" button to close the Internet Options dialog box (Figure 2.2.3).

Step-by-Step Directions for Netscape

Step 1. Go to the "Menu Bar," click on "Edit," and choose "Preferences" (Figure 2.2.4).

Step 2. Click on the "Privacy & Security" arrow and click on Cookies. The Cookies pane will appear to the right (Figure 2.2.5).

Step 3. Choose the options you prefer by clicking on the appropriate radio buttons (Figure 2.2.5).

Step 4. Click the "OK" button to close the "Preferences" dialog box (Figure 2.2.5).

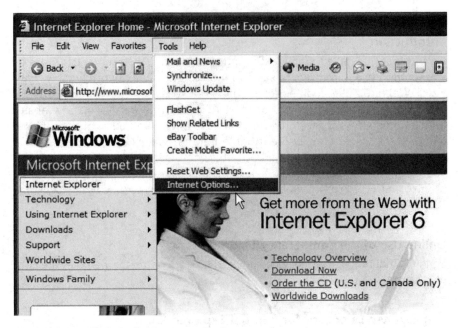

FIGURE 2.2.1 Click Tool > Internet Options.

FIGURE 2.2.2 Click the "Privacy" tab and then the "Advanced . . . " button.

FIGURE 2.2.3 Choose options and click on the "OK" button.

FIGURE 2.2.4 Click on Edit > Preferences.

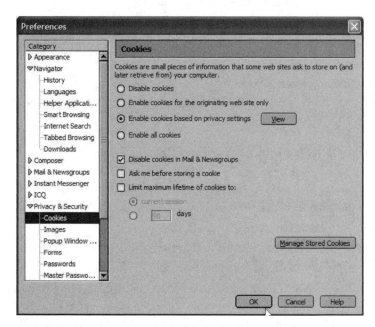

FIGURE 2.2.5 Expand "Privacy & Security" and click on Cookies. Choose options and click the "OK" button.

INTERNET RESOURCES

AOL Webmaster Info, "About Cookies"
http://webmaster.info.aol.com/aboutcookies.html

FindTutorials.com, "What are Cookies"
http://tutorials.findtutorials.com/read//query/enabling%20cookies/id/51

OTHER RELEVANT TUTORIALS

Chapter 2.3: Enabling JavaScript

Chapter 2.19 Setting Security Measures for Your Computer

Chapter 2.6: Adding Plug-ins

Chapter 6.3: Getting Help with Computer Problems

2.3   Enabling JavaScript

Introduction

JavaScript allows for interaction between you and the website you are visiting. Many websites use JavaScript to process forms and verify information. JavaScript is also often used in formatting web pages. If JavaScript is disabled in your browser, pages may not work properly. Interactive items like questionnaires or shopping carts may not work or pages may not display properly.

Online Use of the Competency/Skill

You will understand what JavaScript does and how to enable it in your web browser.

Step-by-Step Directions for Internet Explorer (IE)

Step 1. Go to the "Menu Bar," click on "Tools," and choose "Internet Options" (Figure 2.3.1).

Step 2. Click on the "Security" tab (Figure 2.3.2).

Step 3. Click on "Internet Zone" to highlight (Figure 2.3.2).

Step 4. Click the "Custom Level . . . " button (Figure 2.3.2).

Step 5. Scroll down to the "Scripting" heading (Figure 2.3.3).

Step 6. Click on the "Enable" radio button under the first heading, which is called "Active scripting" (Figure 2.3.3).

Step 7. Click the "OK" button to close the "Security Settings" dialog box (Figure 2.3.3).

Step 8. Click the "OK" button to close the "Internet Options" dialog box.

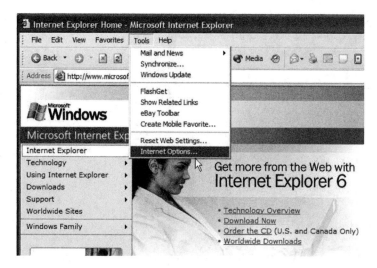

FIGURE 2.3.1 Click Tool > Internet Options.

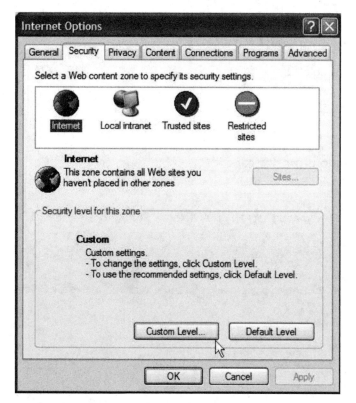

FIGURE 2.3.2 Click "Internet" zone and then the "Custom Level . . . " button.

FIGURE 2.3.3 Click "Enable" under "Active scripting" and then click the "OK" button.

Step-by-Step Directions for Netscape

Step 1. Go to the "Menu Bar," click on "Edit," and choose "Preferences" (Figure 2.3.4).

Step 2. Expand the "Advanced" arrow and click on "Scripts & Plug-ins." The "Scripts & Plug-ins" pane will appear (Figure 2.3.5).

Step 3. Click on the "Navigator" checkbox under "Enable JavaScript for" (Figure 2.3.5).

Step 4. Click the "OK" button to close the Preferences dialog box (Figure 2.3.5).

FIGURE 2.3.4 Click on Edit > Preferences.

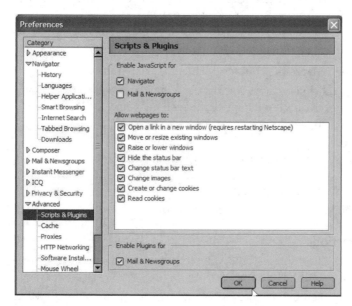

FIGURE 2.3.5 Click "Advanced," "Scripts & Plugins," and then click the "Navigator" checkbox under "Enable JavaScript for." Click the "OK" button.

INTERNET RESOURCES

Internet Related Technologies, "JavaScript Guidelines and Best Practice"
http://www.tech.irt.org/articles/js169/

Tech Encyclopedia, "JavaScript"
http://www.tech-encyclopedia.com/JavaScript.htm

OTHER RELEVANT TUTORIALS

Chapter 2.2: Enabling Cookies
Chapter 2.4: Accessing Web Pages
Chapter 2.6: Adding Plug-ins
Chapter 6.3: Getting Help with Computer Problems

2.4   Accessing Web Pages

Introduction

Learning how to access web pages is essential for the online learner. Here is how accessing a web page works:

- You tell your web browser (IE, Netscape, etc.) to search for a page such as the Yahoo homepage using URL (Uniform Resource Locator), which it translates through HTTP (Hyper Text Transfer Protocol).

- Your computer starts asking your DNS (domain name server) what the IP address of Yahoo is (i.e., http://www.yahoo.com).

- Your web server then reaches out for the IP address in question.

- When one of the other servers recognizes the request (because it has already been there before), it pulls up a copy of the web page and its IP address.

- Your web browser then sends a request for the page using HTTP, and the server responds by sending your web browser the HTML text for the web page, which your browser translates into the web page on your screen.

Online Use of the Competency/Skill

You will have the ability and skill to access web pages.

Step-by-Step Directions

Step 1. From your desktop screen, open the browser that you use most often—Internet Explorer (IE), Netscape, or other.

Step 2. There are numerous ways to access web pages using your browser: entering URLs into the address bar, clicking links from other web pages, clicking bookmarks or favorites, clicking a tab or icon, or searching. Experiment with these ways to access a web page.

Step 3. If you cannot view a specific web page you are trying to open, keep in mind that the reason you can't access a particular web page may not be a problem with your computer. The server for the page may be temporarily down (in which case, you'll have to wait until the server is up again), or the page may be temporarily down (in which case, you'll have to wait until the page is up again), or the page may no longer exist on the Internet. If you get an error message such as "Page Not Found," try the following:

- Try the address a second time.
- URLs must be typed exactly. Ensure case sensitivity (upper or lower case) and avoid extra punctuation, spaces, and other characters if you copy and paste in a URL.
- If you used a hyperlink, press your browser's back button and click again on the hyperlink you used. Or close the error message page and enter or re-enter into your address bar the URL of the page you want.
- Refresh the page. Click on the Refresh (or Reload) button on your browser's toolbar.
- If the above suggestions don't work, try deleting your temporary Internet files, history, and cookies (see your browser Help on how to do so).

INTERNET RESOURCES

Web Teacher, "Web Basics"
http://www.webteacher.org/windows.html

Find Tutorials, "Browsing Web Pages"
http://tutorials.findtutorials.com/read/category/10/id/405

How Stuff Works, "How Internet Search Engines Work"
http://computer.howstuffworks.com/search-engine.htm

Widener University Wolfgang Memorial Library, "Accessing Web Pages Using Netscape"
http://www2.widener.edu/Wolfgram-Memorial-Library/pyramid/wwwawpun.htm

Oracle Think Quest, "Breaking Through the Ice on the Internet"
http://library.thinkquest.org/24114/

OTHER RELEVANT TUTORIALS

Chapter 2.5: Bookmarking Websites and Pages
Chapter 2.12: Copying and Pasting Internet Addresses from Your Screen
Chapter 2.17: Using Two or More Open Programs in Windows
Chapter 4.1: Accessing Your Course Anytime, Anywhere
Chapter 4.2: Saving Course Access Information

2.5   Bookmarking Websites and Pages

Introduction

A bookmark allows you to save a link to websites that you want, or need, to access later. You can add as many bookmarks as you would like, and you can organize your bookmarks in a way that makes sense to you. For example, you might categorize them by class subject, search engines, research paper, online book stores, and financial aid. While they are called Bookmarks in Netscape and Favorites in Internet Explorer, they serve the same function.

Online Use of the Competency/Skill

You will be able to create and organize bookmarks in your browser for websites.

Step-by-Step Directions for adding a favorite in Internet Explorer (IE)

Step 1. Go to the "Menu Bar," click on "Favorites," and choose "Add to Favorites . . . " (Figure 2.5.1).

Step 2. When the "Add Favorite" dialog box pops up, you have two choices:

- Click on the folder that you want to add the bookmark to and then click "OK."
- Click on "OK" without clicking on a folder to add the bookmark to your general favorites category (Figure 2.5.2).

FIGURE 2.5.1 Click Favorites > Add to Favorites.

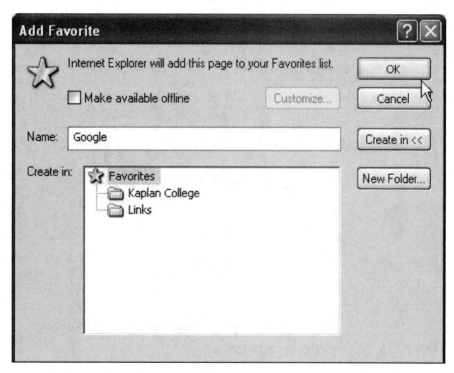

FIGURE 2.5.2 Click on the folder that you want to add the bookmark to, and then click "OK," or just click on "OK."

Step-by-Step Directions for organizing favorites in Internet Explorer

Step 1. Go to the "Menu Bar," click on "Favorites">"Organize Favorites . . ." (Figure 2.5.3).

Step 2. Create a new folder by clicking on "Create Folder" (Figure 2.5.4).

Step 3. Click on the bookmark you want to move and drag it to the folder you want to add it to (Figure 2.5.5).

Step 4. Rename folders by clicking on the folder you want to rename and clicking on "Rename Folder" (Figure 2.5.6).

Step 5. Click on the "Close" button.

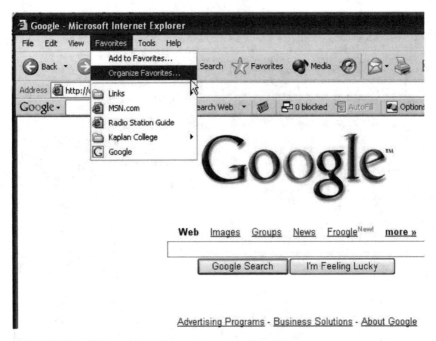

FIGURE 2.5.3 Click on Favorites > Organize Favorites.

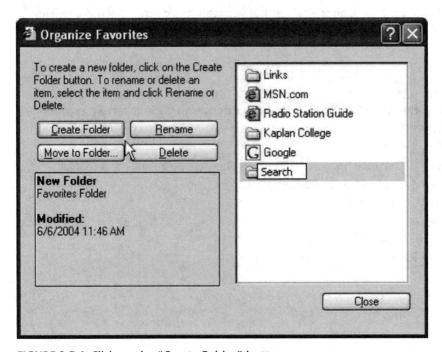

FIGURE 2.5.4 Click on the "Create Folder" button.

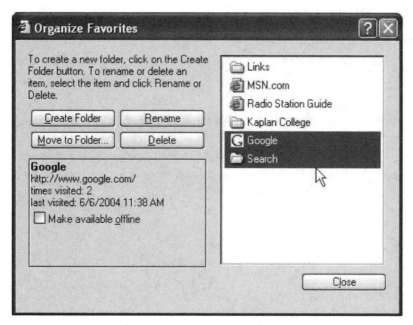

FIGURE 2.5.5 Click on the bookmark you want to move, then drag it to the folder you want to add it to.

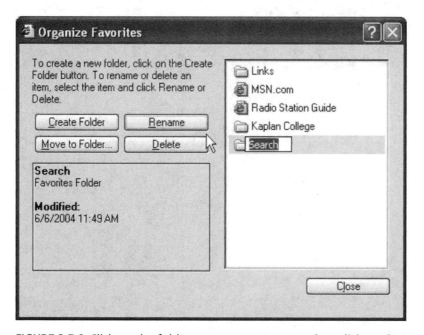

FIGURE 2.5.6 Click on the folder you want to rename, then click on the "Rename" button.

Step-by-Step Directions for adding a bookmark in Netscape

You have several options when you add a bookmark in Netscape:

- To add a bookmark to your general bookmarks, go the "Menu Bar," click on "Bookmarks," and choose "Bookmark This Page" (Figure 2.5.7).
- To add a bookmark to a specific folder:

Step 1. Go to the "Menu Bar," click on "Bookmarks," and choose "File Bookmark . . . " (Figure 2.5.8).

Step 2. In the "Add Bookmark" box, click on the folder you would like to add the bookmark to (Figure 2.5.9).

You may also create a new folder by clicking on the "New Folder . . . " button, type in a name for the new folder, click on the "OK" button, and then choose the new folder (Figure 2.5.9).

Step 3. Click the "OK" button.

FIGURE 2.5.7 Click Bookmarks > Bookmark This Page.

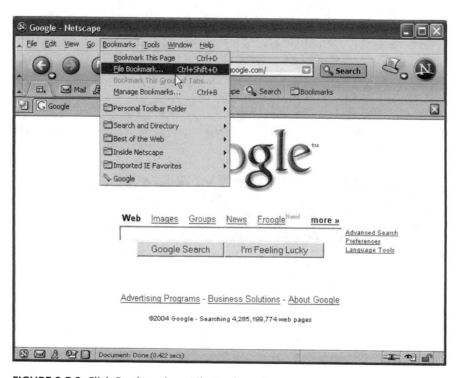

FIGURE 2.5.8 Click Bookmarks > File Bookmark . . .

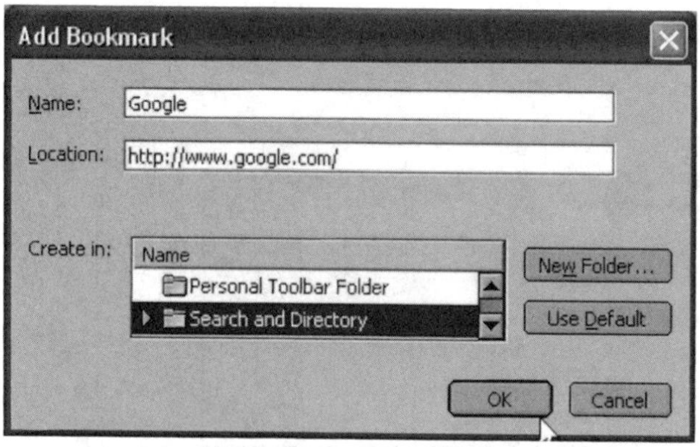

FIGURE 2.5.9 Click on the folder you want to add the bookmark to, then click the "OK" button.

Step-by-Step Directions for managing bookmarks in Netscape

Step 1. Go to the "Menu Bar," click on "Bookmarks," and choose "Manage Bookmarks . . . " (Figure 2.5.10).

Step 2. To move a bookmark to a specific folder, click on the bookmark you want to move, and drag it to the folder you want to add it to (Figure 2.5.11).

Step 3. To close the "Bookmarks" dialog box, go the "Menu Bar, click on "File," and choose "Exit" or click on the "X" in the top right corner of the dialog box (Figure 2.5.12).

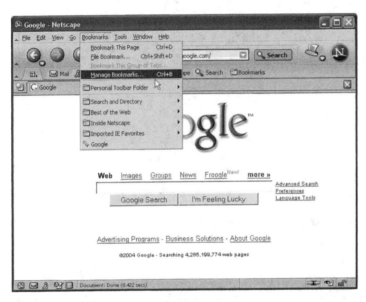

FIGURE 2.5.10 Click Bookmarks > Manage Bookmarks . . .

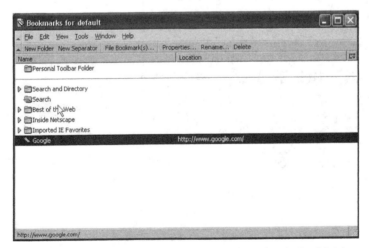

FIGURE 2.5.11 Click and drag the bookmark to the desired folder.

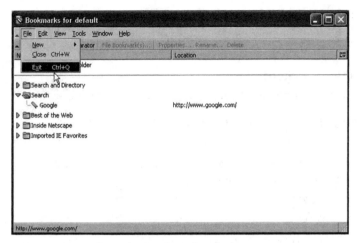

FIGURE 2.5.12 Close the Bookmarks window.

INTERNET RESOURCES

Internet4classrooms, "Using Favorites Effectively"
http://www.internet4classrooms.com/entry_level_pc_ie_fav.htm

Shasta College, "Bookmark a Favorite Website"
http://online.shastacollege.edu/webct/survivalguide/16bookmark.htm

OTHER RELEVANT TUTORIALS

Chapter 2.4: Accessing Web Pages

Chapter 6.3: Getting Help with Computer Problems

2.6   Adding Plug-ins

Introduction

A "plug-in" is a software program that enhances the capabilities of another program. Plug-ins are often associated with web browsers and include the applications listed below. Websites utilizing these technologies will often have a link to the company's website, where you can download the necessary application.

Adobe Acrobat Reader—Allows you to view documents that are in Portable Document Format (.pdf). Webmasters/Organizations will often convert documents created in other applications, such as Microsoft Word, to pdf format because pdf files are usually smaller and anyone can download and install Acrobat Reader for free. You don't need the software that the document was originally created with installed on your computer. Website: http://www.adobe.com

RealPlayer by RealNetworks—Lets you play streaming audio, video, animations, and multimedia presentations on the web. Website: http://www.real.com

Shockwave and Flash Player by Macromedia—Allow you to view and interact with 3D games and entertainment, interactive presentations and demonstrations, and online learning applications. Website: http://www.macromedia.com

Online Use of the Competency/Skill

You will know how to use and install plug-in applications for web browsers.

Step-by-Step Directions for Internet Explorer (IE)

Step 1. Go to the website for the plug-in you want to install.

Step 2. Click on the "Get" button (other websites may direct you to a "Download" button or something similar) (Figure 2.6.1).

Step 3. Answer the website's questions and choose available options.

Step 4. Click the "Download" button (Figure 2.6.2).

Step 5. Click the "Save" button (Figure 2.6.3).

Step 6. Navigate to the folder you would like to save the file in.

Step 7. Click the "Save" button (Figure 2.6.4).

Step 8. Click the "Open" button (Figure 2.6.5).

Step 9. Follow the installation instructions.

The process is the same for Netscape. Different plug-ins may have some minor differences, but the process is basically the same.

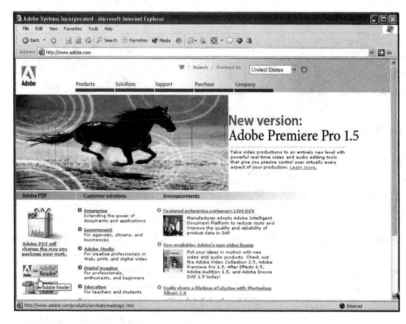

FIGURE 2.6.1 Click on the "Get" button.

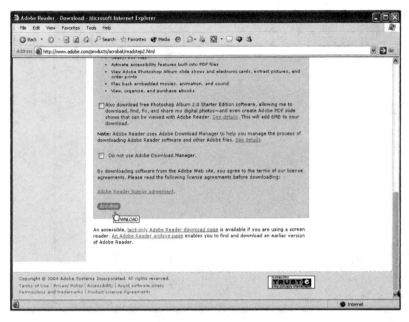

FIGURE 2.6.2 Click on the "Download" button.

FIGURE 2.6.3 Click on the "Save" button.

FIGURE 2.6.4 Click on the "Save" button.

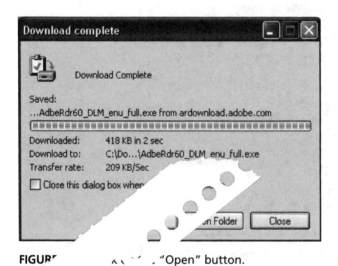

FIGUR⌐   ⌐\ ⌐ ⌐ ⌐ "Open" button.

INTERNET RESOURCES

FindTutorials.com, "Understanding the World Wide Web (Part 1)"
http://tutorials.findtutorials.com/read/query/plug-ins/id/52

Shasta College, "Downloading and Plug-ins"
http://online.shastacollege.edu/webct/survivalguide/19download.htm

OTHER RELEVANT TUTORIALS

Chapter 2.2: Enabling Cookies

Chapter 2.3: Enabling JavaScript

Chapter 6.3: Getting Help with Computer Problems

2.7   Clearing Your Cache

Introduction

When you "surf" the Internet, your browser makes copies of graphics and other content from every page you visit and saves them to your hard drive. This group of files is your "cache" or "Temporary Internet Files." Browsers do this to save time loading pages you have already visited. You might notice that pages you regularly visit load faster than newly visited pages. The increase in speed happens because your browser can pull these previously saved graphics from your cache rather than having to download them over your Internet connection. While this feature can be beneficial, it can be less noticeable with today's higher speed Internet connections. These saved files, however, can use up a lot of hard drive space. To reclaim hard drive space, you should periodically clear your cache.

Online Use of the Competency/Skill

You will understand what your browser is doing "behind the scenes" and know how to conserve your computer's resources.

Step-by-Step Directions for Internet Explorer (IE)

Step 1. Go to the "Menu Bar," click on "Tools," and choose "Internet Options" (Figure 2.7.1).

Step 2. Click on the "Delete Files . . . " button under the "Temporary Internet Files" section (Figure 2.7.2).

Step 3. In the "Delete Files" window, check the "Delete all offline content" checkbox (Figure 2.7.3).

Step 4. Click the "OK" button. The files will be deleted and you will return to the "Internet Options" window (Figure 2.7.3).

Step 5. Click the "OK" button.

FIGURE 2.7.1 Click Tools > Internet Options.

FIGURE 2.7.2 Click on the "Delete Files . . ." button.

FIGURE 2.7.3 Click on the "OK" button.

Step-by-Step Directions for Netscape

Step 1. Go to the "Menu Bar," click on "Edit," and choose "Preferences" (Figure 2.7.4).

Step 2. Click on the "Advanced" arrow and click on "Cache." The "Cache" pane will appear to the right (Figure 2.7.5).

Step 3. Click on the "Clear Memory Cache" button (Figure 2.7.6).

Step 4. Click on the "Clear Disk Cache" button (Figure 2.7.6).

Step 5. Click the "OK" button (Figure 2.7.6).

FIGURE 2.7.4 Edit > Preferences . . .

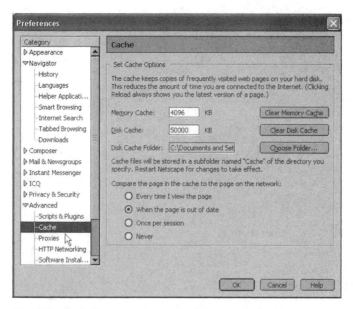

FIGURE 2.7.5 Click on Advanced > Cache.

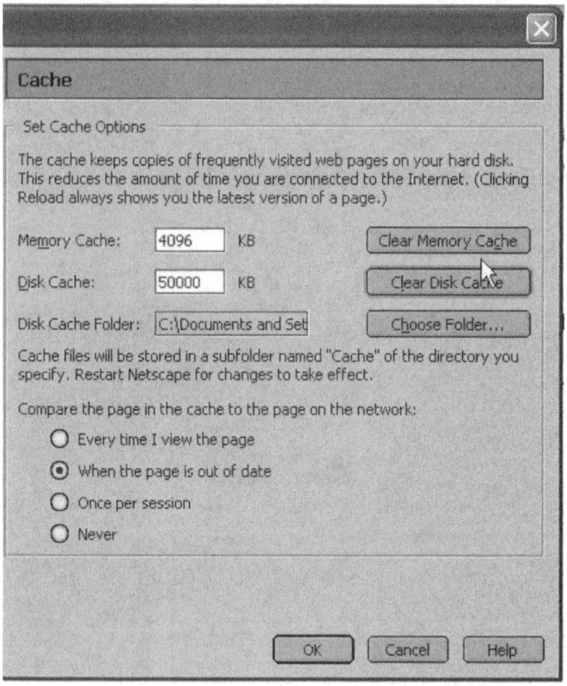

FIGURE 2.7.6 Click the "Clear Memory Cache" button, the "Clear Disk Cache" button, and then the "OK" button.

INTERNET RESOURCES

Cornell University, "Clearing Cache Settings"
http://campusgw.library.cornell.edu/newhelp/technical/errors/answers/clearca
che.html

FindTutorials.com, "Customizing the Browser"
http://tutorials.findtutorials.com/read/query/clearing%20cache/id/407

OTHER RELEVANT TUTORIALS

Chapter 2.2: Enabling Cookies

Chapter 2.3: Enabling JavaScript

Chapter 6.3: Getting Help with Computer Problems

2.8   Setting Computer Monitor Resolution

Introduction

The term "screen resolution" describes the number of "pixels" that your monitor uses to display information. It has no relation to your monitor's physical size. If the resolution is set the same, a 15 inch monitor displays the same information as a 21 inch monitor. The information on the 21 inch monitor will simply be bigger. With a higher resolution, you will see more on the monitor at one time. In general, people are more comfortable using a lower resolution with smaller monitors (640x480 on a 15 inch monitor). With a larger monitor (19 inches or larger), people are often comfortable with a resolution of 1024x768 or higher. Higher resolutions allow more information to be displayed to the user comfortably. The resolution you set your monitor to will depend on the size of your monitor, how much information you want to be displayed at one time and what is comfortable for your vision.

Another consideration, which relates to online learning, is that many website developers are now moving away from optimizing their sites for lower resolutions like 640x480. This is due to more people having larger monitors because of the steadily decreasing cost of these monitors. If you are still using a smaller monitor with a lower resolution, you may find yourself doing more scrolling left and right to view websites.

Online Use of the Competency/Skill

You will know how to set your computer screen resolution.

Step-by-Step Directions for setting your computer screen resolution in Microsoft Windows

Step 1. Right click on the "desktop" and then choose "Properties" (Figure 2.8.1).

Step 2. Click on the "Settings" tab (Figure 2.8.2).

Step 3. Click and drag the "Screen Resolution" slider control left (to decrease resolution) or right (to increase resolution), and then click the "Apply" button (Figure 2.8.3).

Step 4. Click on the "Yes" button in the "Monitor Settings" dialog box and then click "OK" in the "Display Properties" box (Figure 2.8.4).

FIGURE 2.8.1 Right-click on the desktop and then click on "Properties."

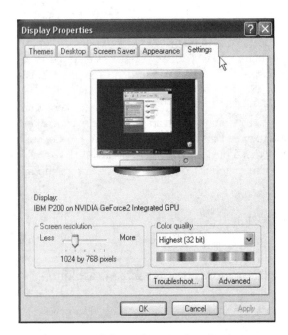

FIGURE 2.8.2 Click on the "Settings" tab.

FIGURE 2.8.3 Click and move the "Screen Resolution" slider control left or right and then click "Apply."

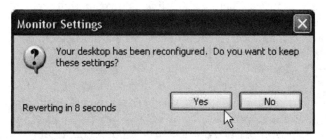

FIGURE 2.8.4 Click "Yes" in the "Monitor Settings" dialog box and then click "OK" in the "Display Properties" box.

INTERNET RESOURCES

About.com, "How to Change Your Windows 2000 Screen Resolution"
http://windows.about.com/c/ht/00/07/How_Change_Windows_2000096293300
4.html

Learnthenet.com, "Master the Basics: Monitor Settings"
http://www.learnthenet.com/english/html/06settng.htm

Microsoft.com, "Windows XP Professional Product Documentation"
http://www.microsoft.com/resources/documentation/windows/xp/allproddocs
/en-us/display_change_screen_resolution.mspx

OTHER RELEVANT TUTORIALS

2.9   Setting Document View with Zoom

Introduction

Most applications, such as word processors and spreadsheets, allow you to view
and edit the documents at a variety of zoom, or magnification, levels. Most likely,
you will find a level of zoom that is comfortable to you in terms of reducing eye
strain and general working comfort. There will be times, however, that you will
be working on a detailed assignment and will want to concentrate on a table
with a lot of information or get an "overall" view of your assignment. Zoom controls the magnification of the document as it appears on your screen, but it does
not affect the printed copy. Microsoft Word often, by default, displays documents
at a zoom level of 100% or at a level that is a best fit for the size of the window
you have open. With a zoom setting of 50%, you will see the whole document
but it will not be very readable. A zoom setting of 200% will display part of the
document but it will be easy to read. Choose a zoom level that is comfortable for
the particular project you are working on.

Online Use of the Competency/Skill

You will know how to set the zoom level of a document.

Step-by-Step Directions for setting the document zoom in Microsoft Word

Step 1. Open a document and observe the current zoom setting (Figure 2.9.1).

Step 2. Click the down arrow next to the zoom selection and change to 50%
(Figure 2.9.2). Notice that you can see the whole page but it is not very clear.

Step 3. Click the down arrow next to the zoom selection and change to 200% (Figure 2.9.3). Notice that you can now see only part of the page but the detail is clear.

The zoom control works in approximately the same way for most other applications.

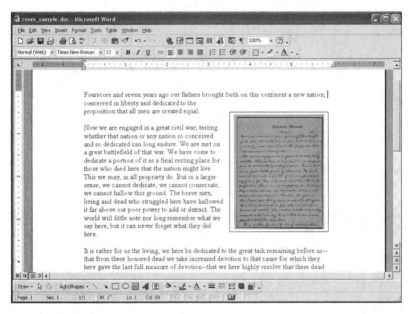

FIGURE 2.9.1 A document at 100% zoom.

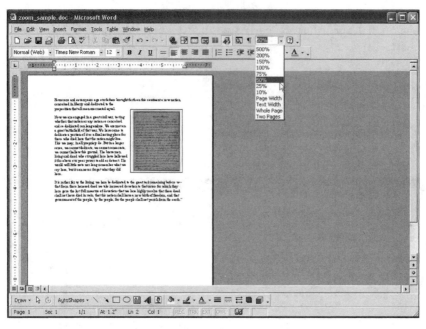

FIGURE 2.9.2 Click the down arrow next to the zoom selection and change to 50%.

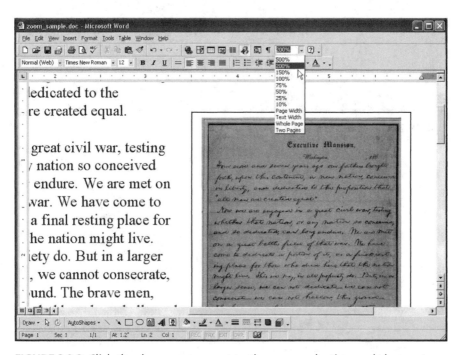

FIGURE 2.9.3 Click the down arrow next to the zoom selection and change to 200%.

Computertim Technologies, "Zoom"
http://www.computertim.com/howto/article.php?topic=word&idn=100

OTHER RELEVANT TUTORIALS

Chapter 2.8: Setting Computer Monitor Resolution
Chapter 6.2: Minimizing Eye Strain
Chapter 6.3: Getting Help with Computer Problems

2.10 Creating Course Folders

Introduction

As an online learner, you will likely take a considerable number of classes, both concurrently and over the course of your education. Many of your assignments will be completed and saved on your computer. Rather than simply saving all of these assignments on your computer's hard drive haphazardly or in one big folder called "School" or some such generic name, it is a good idea to organize those assignments so you can easily find them to work on or refer back to. If you create a folder for each course and save assignments to that folder, it will be easier for you to find your assignments in the future.

Online Use of the Competency/Skill

You will be able to create course folders on your hard drive to keep assignments organized.

Step-by-Step Directions for creating course folders in Microsoft Windows

Step 1. Double-click on "My Computer" (Figure 2.10.1).

Step 2. Click on "Folders" to change to folder view (Figure 2.10.2).

Step 3. Click on "My Documents" to highlight the folder (Figure 2.10.3).

Step 4. Go to the "Menu Bar," click on "File," choose "New," and then choose "Folder" (Figure 2.10.4).

Step 5. Type in a name for the folder and hit Enter (Figure 2.10.5).

Step 6. The new folder will appear in the left pane (Figure 2.10.6).

Step 7. To add a sub-folder, highlight the new folder you just created and repeat the above steps (click File > New > Folder, type a name for that folder, and hit Enter) (Figure 2.10.7).

You can repeat these steps as many times as you need to create folders for each of your courses. You can also start at any point, not necessarily in "My Documents." You can start at the root of your hard drive, floppy disk, or flash drive, for example.

FIGURE 2.10.1 Double-click on "My Computer."

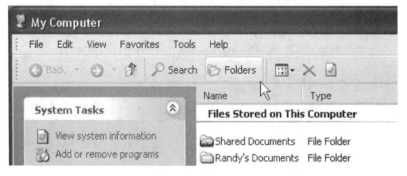

FIGURE 2.10.2 Click on "Folders" to change to folder view.

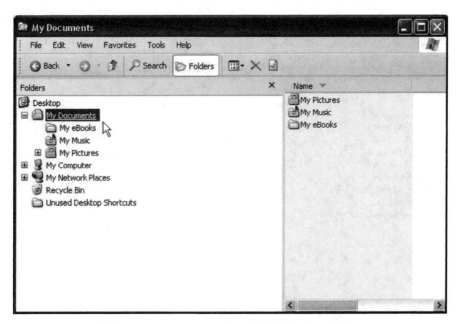

FIGURE 2.10.3 Click on "My Documents" to highlight the folder.

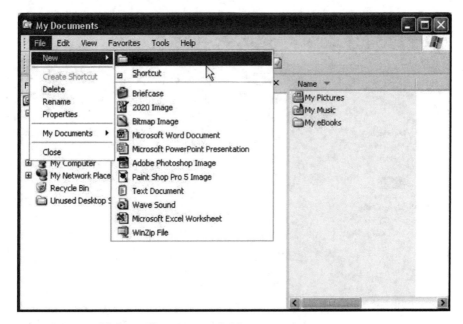

FIGURE 2.10.4 Click on File > New > Folder.

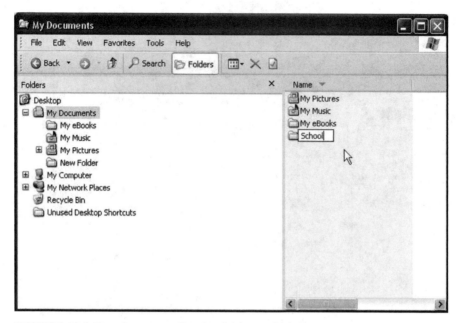

FIGURE 2.10.5 Type in a name for the folder and hit Enter.

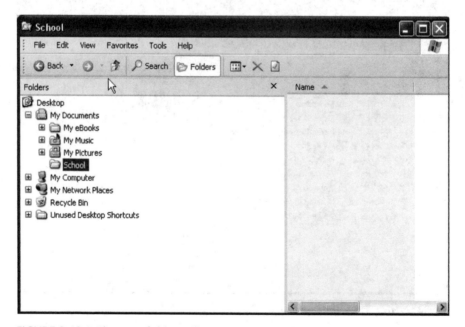

FIGURE 2.10.6 The new folder will appear in the left pane.

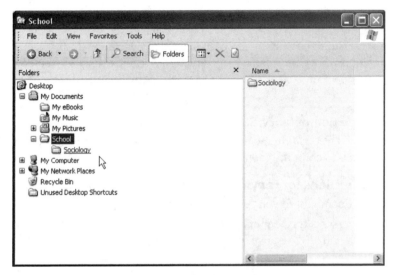

FIGURE 2.10.7 Highlight the new folder, click File > New > Folder, then type a name for that folder and hit Enter.

INTERNET RESOURCES

FindTutorials.com, "Managing Folders"
http://tutorials.findtutorials.com/read/query/creating%20folders/id/466

OTHER RELEVANT TUTORIALS

Chapter 2.14: Saving Files

Chapter 2.15: Uploading Files

Chapter 3.7: Saving Email to Folders

Chapter 6.3: Getting Help with Computer Problems

2.11 Copying and Pasting

Introduction

There will be times, when writing for your classes, that you will want to move or copy text (or tables or graphics) from one part of a document to another part of that document or to another document. This often occurs when writing a rough draft. You have written down a bunch of thoughts and now you want to better organize those thoughts. Rather than retyping those thoughts into new locations, you can "copy" or "cut" words, sentences, pages, and other elements and then "paste" them somewhere. This is one the most powerful features of computer-based word processors and other applications.

You can even copy and paste between applications. For instance, you have found some useful text on a web page and you would like to quote it in your document. You can copy from the website and paste it into your document.Copying text from another source, rather than reading and retyping, will help to ensure accuracy.

Remember: You must cite the work that you copy. You do not want to plagiarize.

Online Use of the Competency/Skill

You will know how to copy or move information from one document to another document or from one computer application to another.

Step-by-Step Directions for copying and pasting in Microsoft Word

Step 1. Create a document in your word processor (Figure 2.11.1).

Step 2. Place the cursor at the beginning of the text that you want to copy, and then click and drag until you have highlighted all that you want to copy (Figure 2.11.2).

Step 3. At this point, there are several ways you can copy:

- You can click on the "Menu Bar," click on "Edit," and choose "Copy" (Figure 2.11.3).
- You can click on the "Copy" icon in the toolbar (Figure 2.11.4).
- You can place the mouse cursor over the highlighted text, "right-click" the mouse, and then choose "Copy" from the pop-up box (Figure 2.11.5).
- You can use the keyboard by pressing Ctrl+C.

Note: When you "Copy," you leave the original text intact. Usually when you are working within a single document, you want to *move* the text from one part of the document to another. To delete the original text, you can use any of methods used above to copy but use Edit > Cut, the "Cut" icon, right-click and select "Cut," or press Ctrl + X. This will delete the original text but you will still be able to paste it where you want it using the following steps.

Step 4. Place the cursor where you would like to insert the text you just copied and left-click your mouse (Figure 2.11.6).

Step 5. You have several choices as to how to paste the text:

- You can go to the "Menu Bar," click on "Edit," and choose "Paste" (Figure 2.11.7).
- You can click on the "Paste" icon in the toolbar (Figure 2.11.8).
- You can right-click the mouse and then choose "Paste" from the pop-up box (Figure 2.11.9).
- You can use the keyboard by pressing Ctrl+V.

The result will be a copy of the text where you want it to be placed (Figure 2.11.10).

These techniques can also be used to "copy and paste" or "cut and paste" between applications. For example, if you have some text in a Word document that you would like to use in a PowerPoint presentation or an Excel spreadsheet, you can copy from the Word document and paste it into your presentation or spreadsheet.

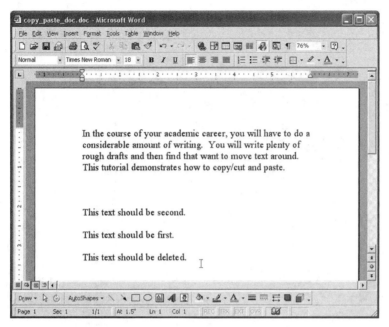

FIGURE 2.11.1 Create a document in your word processor.

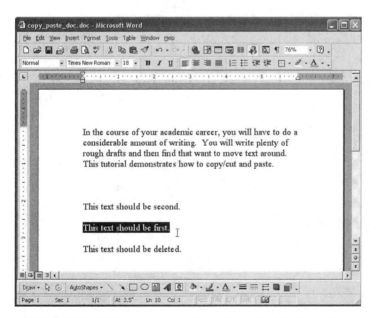

FIGURE 2.11.2 Click and drag until you have highlighted all that you want to copy.

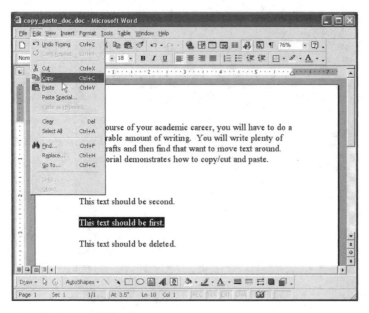

FIGURE 2.11.3 Click Edit > Copy.

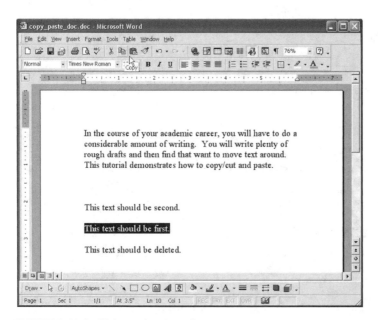

FIGURE 2.11.4 Click on the Copy icon.

FIGURE 2.11.5 Right-click and select "Copy."

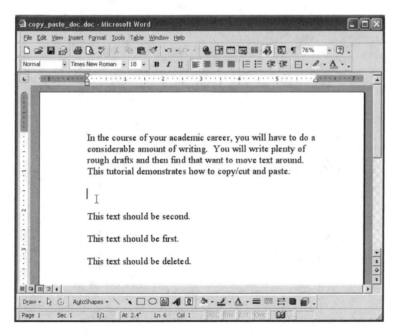

FIGURE 2.11.6 Place the cursor where you want to insert the text.

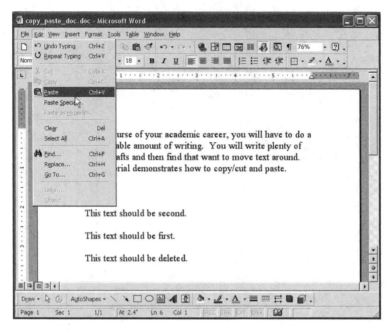

FIGURE 2.11.7 Click Edit > Paste.

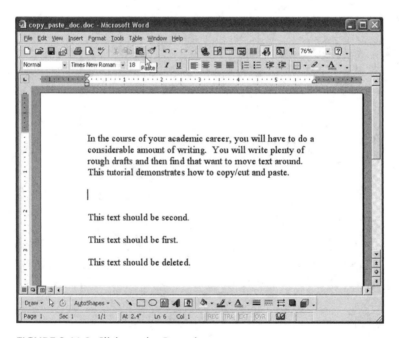

FIGURE 2.11.8 Click on the Paste icon.

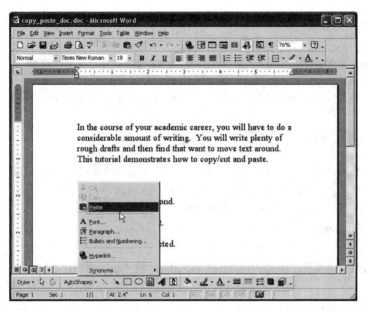

FIGURE 2.11.9 Place the cursor where you want to insert the text, then right-click and select "Paste."

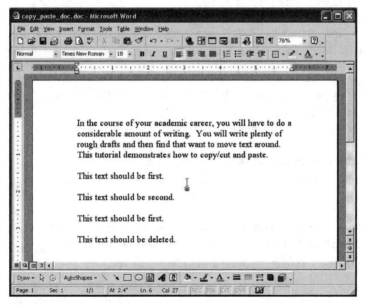

FIGURE 2.11.10 The result will be a copy of the text in the desired place.

INTERNET RESOURCES

DMIA.org, "How to copy and paste"
http://www.dmia.org/tutorial/basic_internet_tut/copy_paste_tut.html

FindTutorials.com, "Word 2002 (XP) Moving and Copying Text"
http://tutorials.findtutorials.com/read/query/copying%20&%20pasting/id/342

OTHER RELEVANT TUTORIALS

Chapter 2.12: Copying and Pasting Internet Addresses from Your Screen

Chapter 2.13: Copying and Pasting from a pdf file (Acrobat Reader)

Chapter 5.6: Recognizing and Avoiding Plagiarism

Chapter 6.3: Getting Help with Computer Problems

2.12   Copying and Pasting Internet Addresses from Your Screen

Introduction

When doing research for assignments, you will often find references to websites. These references will usually be in the form of a Universal Resource Locator (URL) that is a "hyperlink." A hyperlink can be in many forms and have many different uses, but for our discussion, a hyperlink is a link in a document or web page that takes you to another web page when clicked with a mouse. Hyperlinks usually appear as underlined text in a different color from the surrounding text. Sometimes, however, the URL is simply text and nothing happens if you try to click on it. Rather than having to type the link into your browser's address bar (sometimes URLs are long and cryptic), you can copy it from the document and paste it into the address bar.

Conversely, you may also find a website that you would like to use as a reference and wish to include its URL in a document you are creating. You can copy the URL from the address bar to your document.

Online Use of the Competency/Skill

You will know how to copy a URL from a web browser to a document and vice versa.

Step-by-Step Directions for copying a URL from a Microsoft Word document and pasting it into a web browser address bar

Step 1. Open a document that contains a URL (Figure 2.12.1).

Step 2. Place the cursor at the beginning of the text that you want to copy and then click and drag until you have highlighted all that you want to copy (Figure 2.12.2).

Step 3. At this point, there are several ways you can copy:

- You can go the "Menu Bar," click on "Edit," and choose "Copy" (Figure 2.12.3).
- You can click on the "Copy" icon in the toolbar (Figure 2.12.4).
- You can place the mouse cursor over the highlighted text, right-click the mouse, and then choose "Copy" from the pop-up box (Figure 2.12.5).
- You can use the keyboard by pressing Ctrl + C.

Step 4. Delete whatever URL is in the address bar of your browser and place your cursor in the empty address bar (Figure 2.12.6).

Step 5. You have several choices as to how to paste the text:

- You can go to the "Menu Bar," click on "Edit," and choose "Paste" (Figure 2.12.7).
- You can right-click the mouse and then choose "Paste" from the pop-up box (Figure 2.12.8).
- You can use the keyboard by pressing Ctrl + V.

The result will be the URL in the address bar. To go to that website, hit Enter or click on "Go" (Figure 2.12.9).

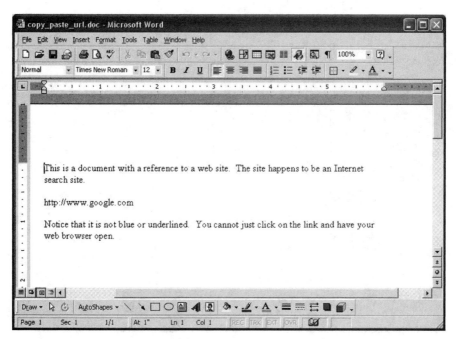

FIGURE 2.12.1 Open a document that contains a URL in your word processor.

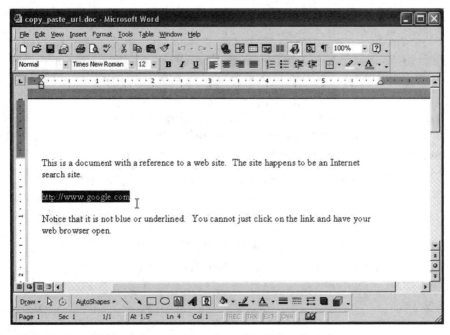

FIGURE 2.12.2 Click and drag until you have highlighted all that you want to copy.

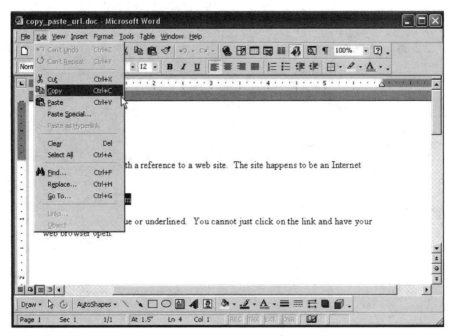

FIGURE 2.12.3 Click Edit > Copy.

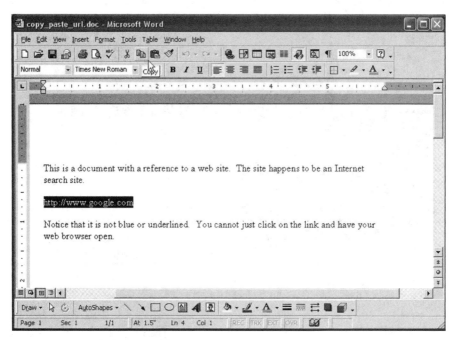

FIGURE 2.12.4 Click on the Copy icon.

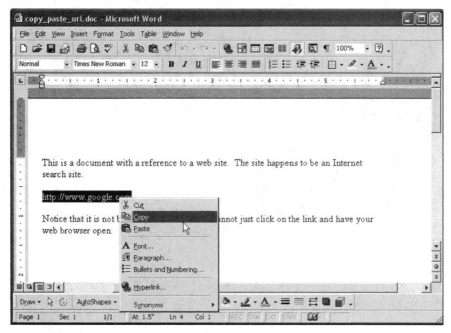

FIGURE 2.12.5 Right-click and select "Copy."

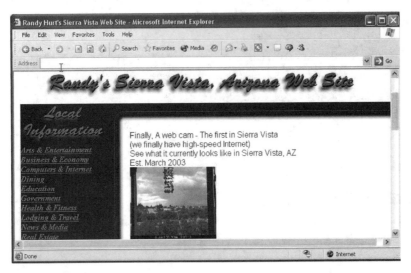

FIGURE 2.12.6 Delete whatever URL is in the address bar of your browser and place your cursor in the empty address bar.

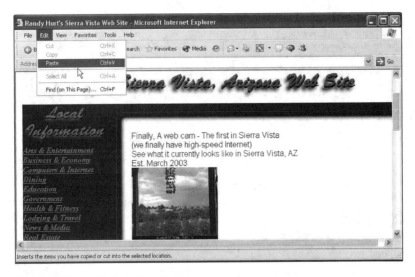

FIGURE 2.12.7 Click Edit > Paste.

FIGURE 2.12.8 Right-click the mouse and select "Paste."

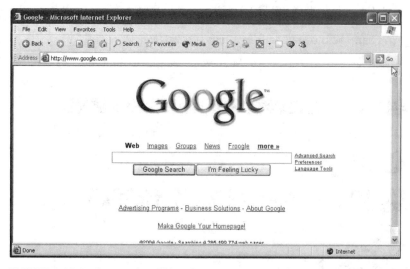

FIGURE 2.12.9 The result will be the URL in the address bar. Hit Enter or click on "Go" to visit the website.

Step-by-Step Directions for copying a URL from a web browser address bar and pasting it into a Microsoft Word document

Step 1. Open your web browser and go to the desired website (Figure 2.12.10).

Step 2. Place the cursor at the beginning of the URL in the address bar and then click and drag until you have highlighted the whole URL (Figure 2.12.11).

Step 3. At this point, there are several ways you can copy:

- You can go to the "Menu Bar," click on "Edit," and choose "Copy" (Figure 2.12.12).
- You can place the cursor over the highlighted text, right-click the mouse, and then choose "Copy" from the pop-up box (Figure 2.12.13).
- You can use the keyboard by pressing Ctrl + C.

Step 4. Open the document that you want to paste the URL into and place the cursor where you want to place the URL (Figure 2.12.14).

Step 5. You have several choices as to how to paste the URL:

- You can go to the "Menu Bar," click on "Edit," and choose "Paste" (Figure 2.12.15).
- You can click on the "Paste" icon in the toolbar (Figure 2.12.16).
- You can right-click the mouse and then choose "Paste" from the pop-up box (Figure 2.12.17).
- You can use the keyboard by pressing Ctrl+V.

The result will be the URL inserted into your document. (Figure 2.12.18).

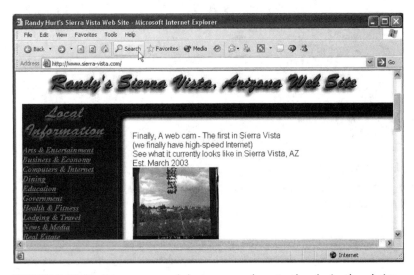

FIGURE 2.12.10 Open your web browser and go to the desired website.

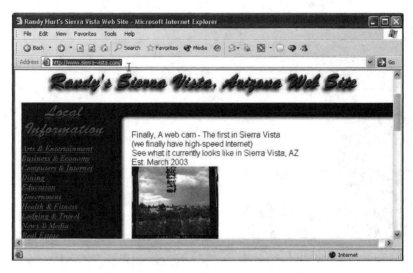

FIGURE 2.12.11 Click and drag until you have highlighted the URL you want to copy.

FIGURE 2.12.12 Click Edit > Copy.

FIGURE 2.12.13 Right-click and select "Copy."

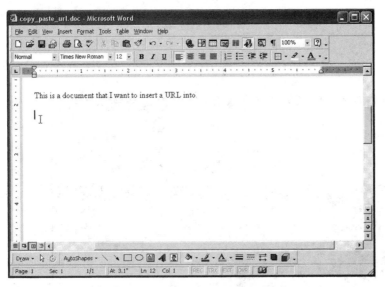

FIGURE 2.12.14 Place the cursor where you want to place the URL.

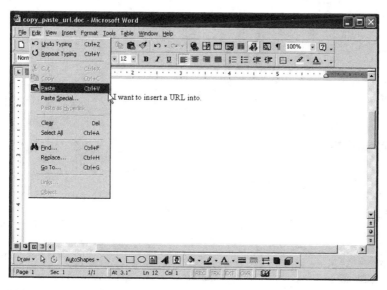

FIGURE 2.12.15 Click Edit > Paste.

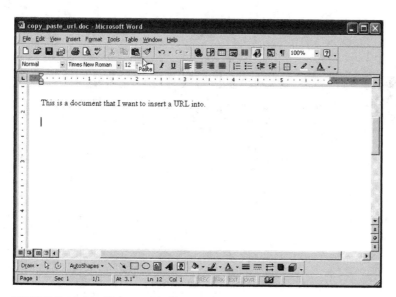

FIGURE 2.12.16 Click on the Paste icon.

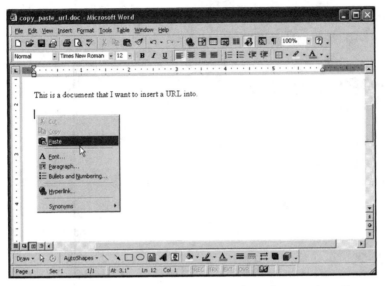

FIGURE 2.12.17 Right-click the mouse and then choose "Paste" from the pop-up box.

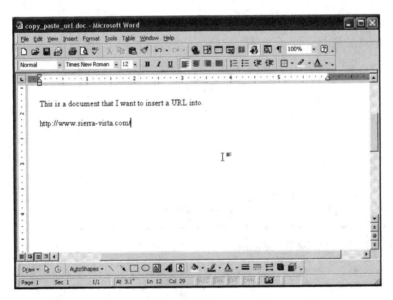

FIGURE 2.12.18 The URL is inserted into your document.

2.13 Copying and Pasting from a pdf file (Acrobat Reader)

Introduction

When doing research for your classes, you may come across documents that are in Portable Document Format (pdf). Many organizations convert documents, created in a variety of applications, to pdf format because of file size reduction, the ability to prevent modification of the document, and portability. Anyone can read a pdf document by simply downloading a free program called Acrobat Reader, available on the Adobe website. Acrobat Reader can be run on any computer platform. Often, you will not be able to simply copy and paste information from a pdf document as you would many other forms of documents. However, Adobe Acrobat Reader provides a tool to select the text you want to copy.

Remember: It is essential to properly cite any information you use. You do not want to plagiarize. Be advised that some pdf documents will be locked and not allow you to copy text.

Online Use of the Competency/Skill

You will know how to use Adobe Acrobat Reader to copy information from a pdf document.

Step-by-Step Directions for copying from a pdf file

Step 1. Open a pdf document in Acrobat Reader.

Step 2. Click on the "Select Text" button on the toolbar (Figure 2.13.1). Once you click on this, your cursor will change from a hand to an "I-beam" cursor.

Step 3. Place the cursor at the beginning of the text that you want to copy and then click and drag until you have highlighted all that you want to copy.

Step 4. At this point, there are several ways you can copy:

- You can go to the "Menu Bar," click on "Edit," and choose "Copy" (Figure 2.13.2).

- You can place the mouse cursor over the highlighted text, right-click the mouse, and then choose "Copy to Clipboard" from the pop-up box (Figure 2.13.3).
- You can use the keyboard by pressing Ctrl + C.

Step 5. Open the other document you want to paste the text to.

Step 6. Place the cursor where you want to paste the text and left-click your mouse.

Step 7. You have several choices as to how to paste the text:

- You can go to the "Menu Bar," click on "Edit" and choose "Paste" (Figure 2.13.4).
- "Right-click" the mouse and then choose "Paste" from the pop-up box (Figure 2.13.5).
- You can use the keyboard by pressing Ctrl + V.

The result will be a copy of the text in the desired place (Figure 2.13.6).

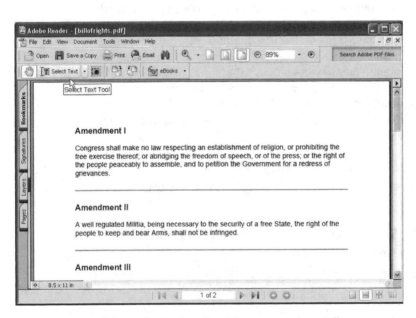

FIGURE 2.13.1 Click on the "Select Text" button on the toolbar.

FIGURE 2.13.2 Click and drag until you have highlighted all that you want to copy. Click on Edit > Copy.

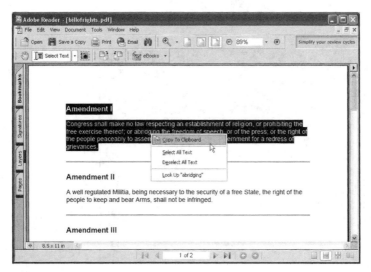

FIGURE 2.13.3 Right-click and select "Copy to Clipboard."

FIGURE 2.13.4 Click Edit > Paste.

FIGURE 2.13.5 Right-click and select "Paste."

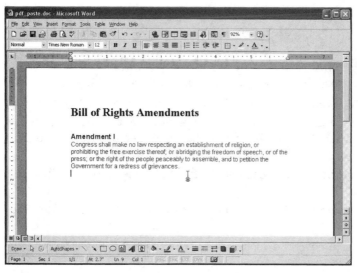

FIGURE 2.13.6 The result will be a copy of the text in the desired place.

OTHER RELEVANT TUTORIALS

Chapter 2.11: Copying and Pasting
Chapter 5.6: Recognizing and Avoiding Plagiarism
Chapter 6.3: Getting Help with Computer Problems

2.14 Saving Files

Introduction

As an online learner, you will have many assignments that you create and save to your computer's hard drive or an external drive. Rather than simply saving all of these assignments on your computer hard drive's root directory (C: or D: drive) or haphazardly in "My Documents," it is a good idea to organize those assignments in a logical way so that you can easily find them for editing, printing, or copying. If you create a folder for each course and save assignments for that course to that folder, it will be easier for you to find course material.

Online Use of the Competency/Skill

You will know how to organize and save files.

Step-by-Step Directions for saving files created in Microsoft Word

Step 1. Create a document in your word processor (Figure 2.14.1).

Step 2. Go to the "Menu Bar," click on "File," and choose "Save" (Figure 2.14.2).

Step 3. Navigate to the folder in which you want to save the document, type a name for the document in the "File name:" box, and then click the "Save" button (Figure 2.14.3).

Step 4. If you do not have a specific folder created, click on the "New Folder" icon (Figure 2.14.4).

Step 5. Type in a name for the new folder and then click on the "OK" button (Figure 2.14.5).

Step 6. Type in a name for the document and then click the "Save" button (Figure 2.14.6).

You can repeat Steps 4 and 5 as many times as you need to create folders that are logical to you. You can also start at any point, not necessarily in "My Documents." You can start at the root of your hard drive, floppy disk, or flash drive, for example.

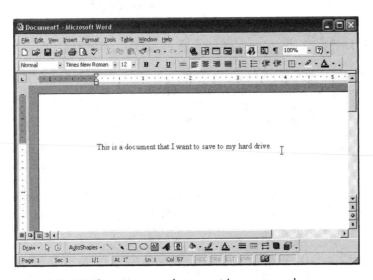

FIGURE 2.14.1 Create a new document in your word processor.

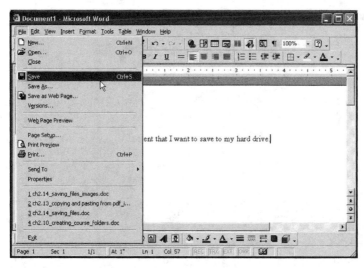

FIGURE 2.14.2 Click File > Save.

FIGURE 2.14.3 Navigate to the desired folder, type in a name, and click "Save."

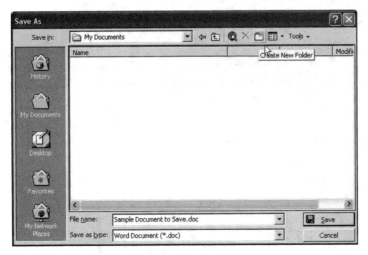

FIGURE 2.14.4 If you do not have a specific folder already, click on the Create New Folder icon.

FIGURE 2.14.5 Type in a folder name and click "OK."

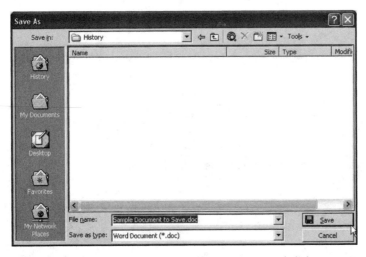

FIGURE 2.14.6 Type in a name for the document and click "Save."

INTERNET RESOURCES

FindTutorials.com, "Windows 2000 Applications (Page 2)"
http://tutorials.findtutorials.com/read/query/saving%20files/id/333/p/2
Web Institute for Teachers, "Computer Basics, All About Windows Specific Information"
http://webinstituteforteachers.org/2000/curriculum/homeroommodules/comp Basics/WinPage.htm#Windows%20on%20Windows

OTHER RELEVANT TUTORIALS

Chapter 2.10: Creating Course Folders
Chapter 2.15: Uploading Files
Chapter 3.7: Saving Email to folders.
Chapter 6.3: Getting Help with Computer Problems

2.15   Uploading Files

Introduction

As an online learner, you will turn assignments in to your instructor electronically. In some cases, you will send assignments to your instructor by attaching them to emails. In other instances, you will be using Blackboard, WebCT, eCollege, or some other web-based online learning application to turn in assignments. Within these applications, there are tools that allow you to upload files to a server where the instructor can retrieve them.

Online Use of the Competency/Skill

You will be able to upload files to a server on the Internet.

Step-by-Step Directions

Step 1. Navigate to the page in your particular online learning application where you can upload assignments. You will usually find a text entry box and a "Browse" (or something similar) button (Figure 2.15.1).

Step 2. Click on the "Browse" button (Figure 2.15.1).

Step 3. Navigate to the folder where the file is that you want to upload, then click on the file name to highlight it. The file name will appear in the "File Name" field. Click on the "Open" button (Figure 2.15.2).

Step 4. The path to your file and the file name itself will appear in the text box (Figure 2.15.3). Click the button labeled "OK," "Upload," "Send," or something similar.

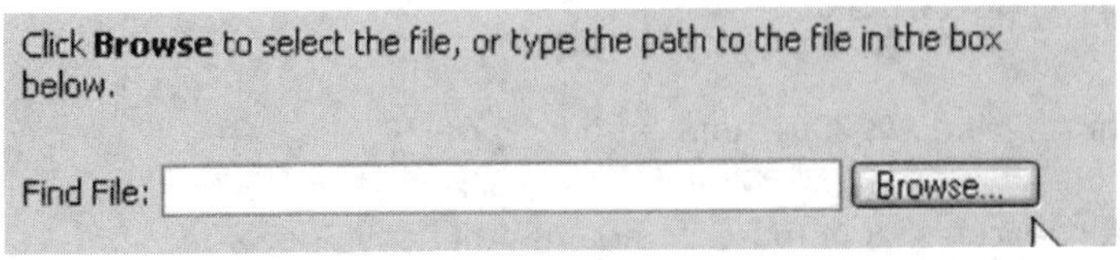

Click **Browse** to select the file, or type the path to the file in the box below.

Find File: [   ] [Browse...]

FIGURE 2.15.1 You will be presented with a text entry field similar to this.

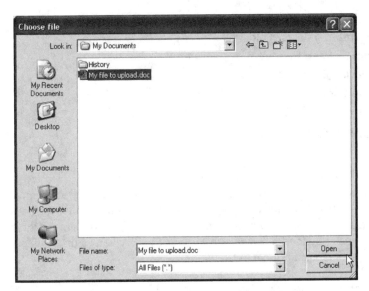

FIGURE 2.15.2 Navigate to the folder where the file is that you want to upload, click on the file, and then click "Open."

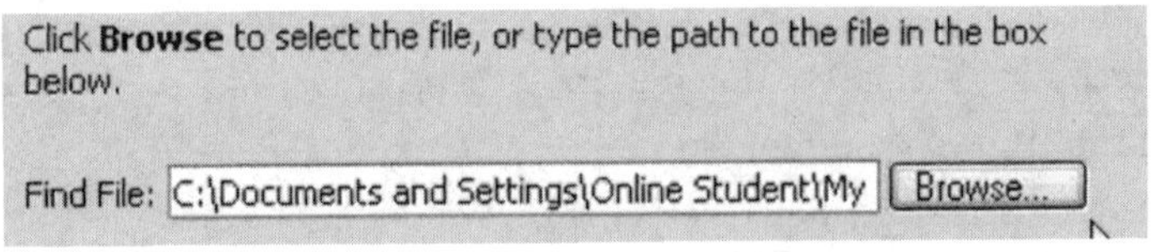

Click **Browse** to select the file, or type the path to the file in the box below.

Find File: [C:\Documents and Settings\Online Student\My] [Browse...]

FIGURE 2.15.3 The path to your file will appear in the text box. Click the button labeled "Upload" or "Send" or something similar.

Uploading Files in Discussion Forums
http://oregonstate.edu/instruct/pte/tutorial/forums/attach.htm

OTHER RELEVANT TUTORIALS

Chapter 2.14: Saving Files
Chapter 3.8: Attaching Files to Email
Chapter 6.3: Getting Help with Computer Problems

2.16 Converting to Rich Text Format

Introduction

As an online learner, you will need to create documents in the format that your instructor requests. This may not be a problem you will run into often. However, a situation could come up where you don't have the same word processor as the instructor. Maybe you use WordPerfect but the instructor uses Microsoft Word and you don't have the funds, or desire, to purchase that word processor. One way to work with this situation would to be to create your document in your word processor and then convert it to Rich Text Format (rtf). All rtf files are "portable" in that they can be read by a variety of word processors. This might also be helpful if you do not know what application the person receiving your document will use.

Online Use of the Competency/Skill

You will know how to convert a document to rtf format so that it can be read by different applications.

Step-by-Step Directions

Step 1. Create a document in your word processor (Figure 2.16.1).

Step 2. Go to the "Menu Bar," click "File," and choose "Save As . . . " (Figure 2.16.2).

Step 3. In the "Save As" dialog box, navigate to where you want to save the document (Figure 2.16.3).

Step 4. In the "File name:" box, type in a name for your document (Figure 2.16.3).

Step 5. In the "Save as type:" drop-down box, choose Rich Text Format (*.rtf) (Figure 2.16.3).

Step 6. Click the "Save" button (Figure 2.16.4).

Your word processor will add the .rtf extension to your document.

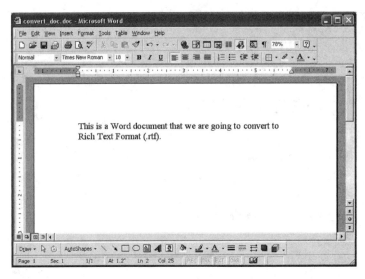

FIGURE 2.16.1 Create a document in your word processor.

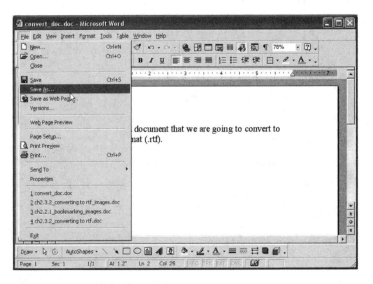

FIGURE 2.16.2 Click File > Save As . . . .

FIGURE 2.16.3 Navigate to where you want to save the document, type in a name for the document, and choose Rich Text Format (*.rtf).

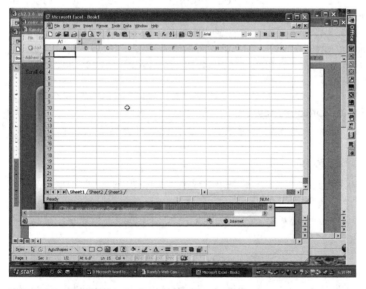

FIGURE 2.16.4 Click on the "Save" button.

INTERNET RESOURCES

Indiana University, "In Microsoft Word and Corel WordPerfect for Windows, what file formats can I save in and convert from?"
http://kb.indiana.edu/data/ahkn.html

Ohio University, "Converting Documents"
http://www.ohiou.edu/independent/tutorial/C_c.htm

Wellesley College, "Opening and Saving documents in various formats with Microsoft Word"
http://www.wellesley.edu/Computing/Word/Conversion/wordToOther.html

OTHER RELEVANT TUTORIALS

Chapter 2.10: Creating Course Folders
Chapter 2.14: Saving Files
Chapter 6.3: Getting Help with Computer Problems

2.17   Using Two or More Open Programs in Windows

Introduction

Often you will want to view more than one program on your computer screen at a time. Most environments, like Microsoft Windows, offer a variety of ways to view and navigate between multiple programs or applications running on your computer. Each program runs in a window, and the various windows can be viewed one at a time. You can navigate between the windows using the mouse or the keyboard.

Online Use of the Competency/Skill

You will be able to use multiple programs in a Windows environment.

Step-by-Step Directions

Step 1. Open several programs so that you have multiple windows open on your computer screen (Figure 2.17.1).

Step 2. Arrange the open windows on your screen. There are several ways you can do this:

- You can cascade the windows by right-clicking on the Task Bar and then clicking "Cascade Windows" (Figure 2.17.2).
- You can tile the windows horizontally by right-clicking on the Task Bar and then clicking "Tile Windows Horizontally" (Figure 2.17.3).
- You can tile the windows vertically by right-clicking on the Task Bar and then clicking "Tile Windows Vertically" (Figure 2.17.4).

- You can minimize all open windows by pressing and holding the "Windows" key and then pressing the "M" key.
- You can then maximize all open windows by pressing and holding the "Windows" key, then pressing the "Shift" key, and then pressing the "M" key.

Step 3. View one open window at a time. Although tiling a couple of open windows can be convenient for copying and pasting between applications, tiling all of the open windows can be awkward to use. You will often want to have several applications running in separate windows at the same time, but you will most likely need only one visible at a time. There are a couple of ways to navigate between the windows.

- You can minimize, and restore, an individual window by clicking on its label in the Task Bar (Figure 2.17.5).
- You can alternate between open windows by pressing and holding the "Alt" key and then pressing the "Tab" key. A window will pop up in the middle of the screen that displays an icon for each open window/application. Each touch of the "Tab" key will highlight a different application. Release the "Tab" key and then the "Alt" key to bring up the desired application.

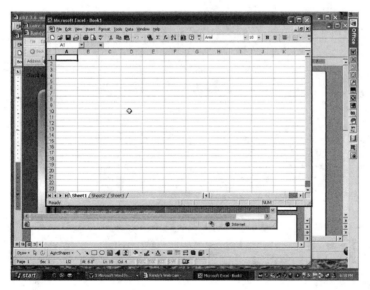

FIGURE 2.17.1 A display with multiple windows open.

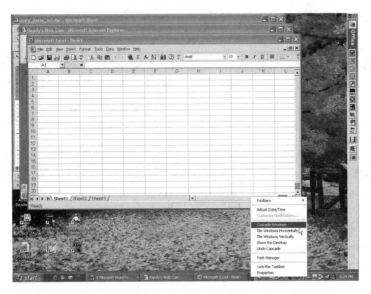

FIGURE 2.17.2 Right-click on the Task Bar and click "Cascade Windows."

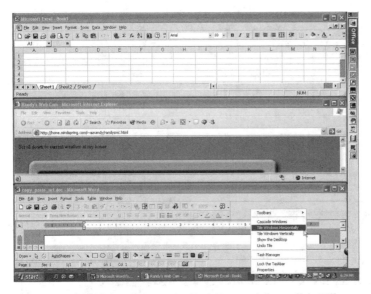

FIGURE 2.17.3 Right-click on the Task Bar and then click "Tile Windows Horizontally."

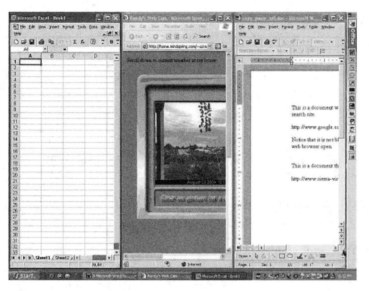

FIGURE 2.17.4 Right-click on the Task Bar and then click "Tile Windows Vertically."

FIGURE 2.17.5 Minimize and maximize a window by clicking on its label in the Task Bar.

INTERNET RESOURCES

Computertim Technologies, "Switch Between Applications"
http://www.computertim.com/howto/article.php?topic=windows&idn=53

Web Institute for Teachers, "Computer Basics, All About Windows Specific Information"
http://webinstituteforteachers.org/2000/curriculum/homeroommodules/comp Basics/WinPage.htm#Windows%20on%20Windows

OTHER RELEVANT TUTORIALS

Chapter 2.4: Accessing Web Pages

Chapter 6.3: Getting Help with Computer Problems

2.18   Protecting Your Computer from Viruses

Introduction

Computer viruses are small programs, usually written with malicious intent, that attach themselves to other programs or files. Viruses will often infect programs in a computer and then replicate themselves and spread to other files and other computers, infecting them as well. Computer viruses can range from being fairly harmless to very destructive. They can cause harmless, but annoying, messages to pop-up on your screen, or they can crash your computer. In the worst case, you could lose hours of hard work. While there is no way to completely immunize your computer from all viruses, you can take some basic steps to protect your system.

Online Use of the Competency/Skill

You will know how to protect your computer from viruses.

Step-by-Step Directions

There are several things you can do to protect your system. These need not be in any particular order. Some may or may not apply to you, depending on what you do with your computer.

Step 1. Protect your computer with anti-virus software, such as McAfee or Norton Anti-virus.

- Have anti-virus software loaded and running on your computer.
- Be sure that you have the latest virus definition files from the anti-virus software vendor. Most anti-virus software can be configured to automatically check to see that you have the most up-to-date definitions.
- When a message pops up asking if you want to check for new definition files or if it informs you that new ones are available for upload, do it! You may be in a hurry or it may seem to be a hassle, but it will cost many times more time and grief if your system crashes or you lose data due to a virus that could have been prevented.

Step 2. Use caution when you download from the Internet. Many viruses are passed through the Internet. You should only download files from reputable sites that you can trust.

Step 3. Virus-check files transferred from other computers. If someone gives you a disk with something on it, or if you put a floppy disk, USB memory device, or CD-R in someone else's computer and copy files to it, scan it with your anti-virus software. This is a particularly good practice in the case of public computers, like those at the library or an Internet cafe.

Step 4. Check that you have the latest patches and updates for your anti-virus software. Most vendors periodically provide updates and patches to their software. Microsoft, for example, provides free updates and patches to their Windows operating system (and other applications, like their Office products) to fix security vulnerabilities that have been found since the software's release. Check vendor websites regularly for updates or patches.

Step 5. Use caution with email attachments. Before opening an attachment to an email, make sure you know what it is and who sent it. If you get an email with an attachment from someone you know, and you were not expecting an attachment from that person, then contact that person by email or phone and find out what the attachment is before you open it.

Step 6. Back up your data. Since you cannot make your computer entirely immune to viruses, back up your important data. Use a tape backup system, CD-R, floppy disks, another computer, or some other system. It is heart wrenching to lose hours of hard work. No time is good for this to happen, but one of the worst times is just before you need to turn in an assignment—and online instructors are becoming less tolerant of students using computer problems as an excuse for not turning in work on time.

INTERNET RESOURCES

Arizona State University, "Securing Your Workstation"
http://www.west.asu.edu/it/start/wksecurity.htm

Carnegie Mellon University, CERT Coordination Center, "Home Computer Security"
http://www.cert.org/homeusers/HomeComputerSecurity/

Wellesley College, "Securing Your Computer"
http://www.wellesley.edu/Computing/Security/

OTHER RELEVANT TUTORIALS

Chapter 2.19: Setting Security Measures for Your Computer
Chapter 3.9: Protecting Your Computer from Email Viruses
Chapter 6.3: Getting Help with Computer Problems

2.19   Setting Security Measures for Your Computer

Introduction

Computers, particularly those that are connected to networks, and especially those connected to the Internet, are vulnerable to attacks from viruses and hackers. To keep your computer, and the data stored on it, as safe as possible, you need to take some basic steps to provide protection from these threats.

Online Use of the Competency/Skill

You will be able to increase security on your computer.

Step-by-Step Directions

There are several things you can do to help keep your computer secure. These need not be in any particular order. Some may or may not apply to you, depending on what you do with your computer.

Step 1. Install and keep your anti-virus software up to date. New viruses are discovered nearly every day, and they can propagate extremely fast. Run virus scans on your hard drive often, or configure the software to run automatically at set intervals.

Step 2. Ensure that you have the latest software updates and patches. Hackers can exploit vulnerabilities to hack into your computer and, in the worst case, steal or destroy important information or crash your system and make it inoperable. Check to see that you have the latest updates and patches for your operating system, web browser, and other software. Microsoft, for example, often has updates and patches to fix security vulnerabilities. If you are using Microsoft products, you can set up your computer to automatically check for updates for the operating system, web browser, and other software.

Step 3. Keep your computer free of adware and spyware. Adware and spyware can be in the form of cookies or hidden programs. These can track your web browsing and report to advertisers or other interested parties. They may also randomly display pop-up windows whether you are web browsing or not. These programs can be annoying, and they can negatively affect your computer's performance. They also cause concern about Internet privacy. Spybot (http://www.safer-networking. org/en/index.html) and Ad-aware (http://www.lavasoftusa.com/software/adaware/) are two of the free programs that can find and remove these programs and cookies.

Step 4. Keep your log-in names or user IDs and passwords safe:

- Create passwords that are cryptic. Mix up letters, numerals, and special characters such as: #@$%^&*.
- Do not use family member names, birth dates, words that are found in the dictionary, or other easily identified text.
- It is best not to write passwords down, but if you do, keep them in a secure place. Under your keyboard is not a secure location.
- Don't have your computer remember your information; enter it manually each time.
- Change your password regularly. Many experts recommend changing passwords once a month.

Step 5. Use sound web browser security practices:

- When you visit a website that requires a log-in and password, be sure that the connection to that site is secure. Two ways to tell are by looking at the URL in the address bar and at an icon at the bottom of your browser. A secure URL will begin with *https* rather than just *http*. Most browsers will display a small icon of a closed padlock at the bottom of the window when the connection is secure.
- Make sure your web browser uses 128-bit encryption for connections to secure websites. If your browser does not support this high encryption, the vendor's website should have a download to fix this.
- When you have finished your business at a website where you had to log in, be sure to log out of the site.
- For additional security, close your browser. This will ensure that the connection is closed.

Step 6. Beware of spoof email and phishing scams. Spoof emails are emails that appear to be from sites like eBay, PayPal, Citibank, or some other reputable site. They attempt to get you to enter your user ID (userid) and password so they can steal them. This type of scam is commonly called phishing. These emails have gotten very sophisticated and look genuine. Most companies will not ask you to enter your access information through an email. They will direct you to their website to log in if they need you to. The best practice is to never do this.

The people who create these emails realize that people are learning about these scams, so they are directing the recipients to forged websites. Although the link in the email may appear to be a legitimate URL, the underlying code may direct you to some other site. If you follow one of these links and the URL in the address bar of your browser is different, be suspicious. Look at the URL carefully. The base domain name should be the name you expect. Even small variations can mean a forged website. If you are directed to mybank.com, be sure mybanks.com or my_bank.com is not the address you see.

If you have any question about the authenticity of the email, go the company's website and look for a link to their security department. They will usually have an email address that you can forward the suspect email to. They will let you know if it is legitimate or a scam.

Step 7. Install a firewall. A firewall is a system (hardware, software, or both) that is used to prevent unauthorized Internet users from accessing private networks or computers that are connected to the Internet. All traffic coming in and going out passes through the firewall. If the traffic does not meet certain criteria, it is blocked. An example of a personal firewall is ZoneAlarm (http://www.zonelabs.com).

Step 8. Always back up your work by saving to an external hard drive, CD-R, or other external storage device.

INTERNET RESOURCES

Arizona State University, "Securing Your Workstation"
http://www.west.asu.edu/it/start/wksecurity.htm

Carnegie Mellon University, CERT Coordination Center, "Home Computer Security"
http://www.cert.org/homeusers/HomeComputerSecurity/

Wellesley College, "Securing Your Computer"
http://www.wellesley.edu/Computing/Security/

OTHER RELEVANT TUTORIALS

Chapter 2.18: Protecting Your Computer from Viruses
Chapter 3.9: Protecting Your Computer from Email Viruses
Chapter 6.3: Getting Help with Computer Problems

CHAPTER 3
Online Email Tasks for Online Learning

Introduction

This chapter focuses on the most essential communication tool in online learning—email. There are twelve email tasks which will empower your ability to communicate effectively. Among the most basic are accessing email, creating emails, and maintaining your email account. Email is a very effective and powerful communication tool. Learning the twelve email skills in this chapter will greatly enhance your online course success.

Some institutions may provide you with an email account. Check with your institution for information on their email policies and procedures. Remember that using email in the context of a college course is very different from sending email to friends and relatives. Be a professional student and pay attention to details, build positive online relationships, and adhere to the standards and etiquette established by your college and instructor.

3.1 Using Email Effectively in Online Courses

Introduction

Email is one of the most used forms of communication today. Compared to other communication media such as the telephone, radio, and television, email remains a relatively new invention. Email is an essential communication tool for distance education. Email is one of the most important tools for communicating with classmates and your instructor. Email communication is about staying connected with your course and college.

Online Use of the Competency/Skill

You will be able to use email for effective communication as an online learner.

Step-by-Step Directions

Step 1. Create an email address. Most Internet providers will allow you one or more email addresses. Some students may want to create an alternative email address through a generic email provider like Hotmail.com, Yahoo.com, or Netscape.net. Be aware that many colleges and universities offer their students a free email account and require students to use that email address for all school communication.

Step 2. If your email account requires a username and password to access, save the information in a safe place. Save as a unique file to your hard drive and on an external device like a diskette, CD-R, or flash drive.

Step 3. Organize your email account in a way that will help you be an efficient online student.

Step 4. Build up your email address book with those email addresses and contacts that will help you stay well connected to your course and college.

Step 5. Discipline yourself to check your email at least every other day, and target responding to email within 24 to 48 hours. Your email is a reflection of you and represents you. Be a professional student.

Step 6. Learn all the email skills and strategies discussed in this chapter.

INTERNET RESOURCES

Learnthenet.com, "Harness Email"
http://www.learnthenet.com/english/section/email.html

Web Teacher, "Communication"
http://www.webteacher.org/windows.html

Kaitlin Sherwood's "A Beginner's Guide to Effectively Using Email"
http://www.webfoot.com/advice/email.top.html

GCF Global Learning, "Email Basics"
http://www.gcflearn.org/en/course/course_detail.asp?Course_ID=19&
Course_Title=Email+Basics

OTHER RELEVANT TUTORIALS

All the tutorials in this chapter.

3.2   Accessing Email

Introduction

Access to your email is critical to maintain communication with fellow students, your instructor, and your school. It is important to access your email account several times a week. You can do so not just from your home computer, but any computer. One of the great values of distance education is the ability to access your course and your email from anywhere at anytime.

Online Use of the Competency/Skill

You will be able to assure access to your email account so that you can stay connected to your course, instructor, and fellow students.

Step-by-Step Directions

Step 1. Create a word document file to write down the information you need to access your email account. Do not trust your memory. Write down the following essentials:

- Your user name
- Your password
- URL for your web-based email account. Chances are you already have an account with a free web-based email service. These email accounts can be accessed from any computer connected to the web, such as the computer in your friend's beach villa on Barbados or the Internet Cafe in Edinburgh, Scotland, or a Kinko's, Starbucks, or your local library.

Step 2. Save as a unique file to your hard drive and on an external device like a diskette, CD-R, or flash drive.

Step 3. Print out all this pertinent information so you can have it as a hard copy and put it into a file folder you have created for your course.

Step 4. Carry with you at all times this important information which will help you stay connected. One idea is to have such important files on a flash drive.

INTERNET RESOURCES

Learnthenet.com, "Harness Email"
http://www.learnthenet.com/english/section/email.html

Web Teacher, "Communication"
http://www.webteacher.org/windows.html

Kaitlin Sherwood's "A Beginner's Guide to Effectively Using Email"
http://www.webfoot.com/advice/email.top.html

GCF Global Learning, "Email Basics"
http://www.gcflearn.org/en/course/course_detail.asp?Course_ID=19&Course_Title=Email+Basics

OTHER RELEVANT TUTORIALS

All the tutorials in this chapter.

3.3 Identifying the Sender (you) and Subject

Introduction

Email has become an important and common form of communication. You probably use email to communicate with your instructors, colleagues, friends, and family. Your instructors can easily receive hundreds of legitimate emails per week. Add to these all of the junk email, or spam, and that number can grow incredibly fast. Because of this large quantity of email, it is important to make email you send as easy to identify as possible. You can do this with meaningful display names and subject lines.

By default, many email applications show your email address as the person an email is from. If you send an email to your instructor and your email address is xyz123@onlinemailprovider.com, your instructor may not be able to tell who sent it if he or she is not familiar with your address. It would be more useful if the "From" field had your actual name. Most email applications allow you to modify the field called "Display Name" (or something similar). This display name field is where you can put in your name. You can type in just about anything, but it is best to use your actual name. "Super Student" or other such phrases can be irritating to recipients and hinder their ability to identify quickly who sent it.

Always include a meaningful subject line in your message. Some useful information for an online student to include might be the class, assignment, and student name: ENG101, Paper #1, Jim Student. Your instructor may have you add something like "***Help***" if you need a quick response. Ask your instructor if you should use a particular format. If you reply to an email but wish to change the subject, you should also change the subject line. Better yet, create a new email with the new subject. The subject line is usually the easiest way to follow the conversation and for filing, so changing the conversation without changing the subject will be confusing.

Online Use of the Competency/Skill

You will be able to create meaningful display names and useful subject lines.

Step-by-Step Directions for setting your display name in Microsoft Outlook

Step 1. Go to the "Menu Bar," click on "Tools," and choose "Accounts" (Figure 3.3.1).

Step 2. Click on your email account name to highlight it and then click on the "Properties" button (Figure 3.3.2).

Step 3. Type your information in the "Name" field and then click the "OK" button (Figure 3.3.3).

Step-by-Step Directions for setting your display name in Hotmail

Step 1. Once you are logged in to your email, click on "Options" (Figure 3.3.4).

Step 2. Click on the "Personal" tab (Figure 3.3.5).

Step 3. Enter your first and last name in the corresponding fields (Figure 3.3.6).

Step 4. Click the "Continue" button (Figure 3.3.7).

Step 5. Send yourself an email to view results (Figure 3.3.8).

FIGURE 3.3.1 Click on Tools > Accounts.

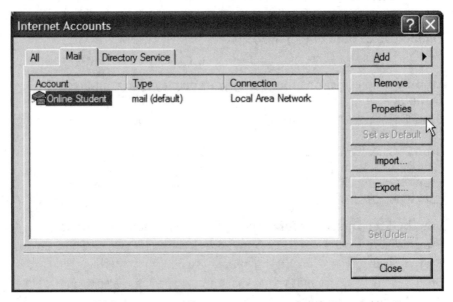

FIGURE 3.3.2 Highlight your email account name and click "Properties."

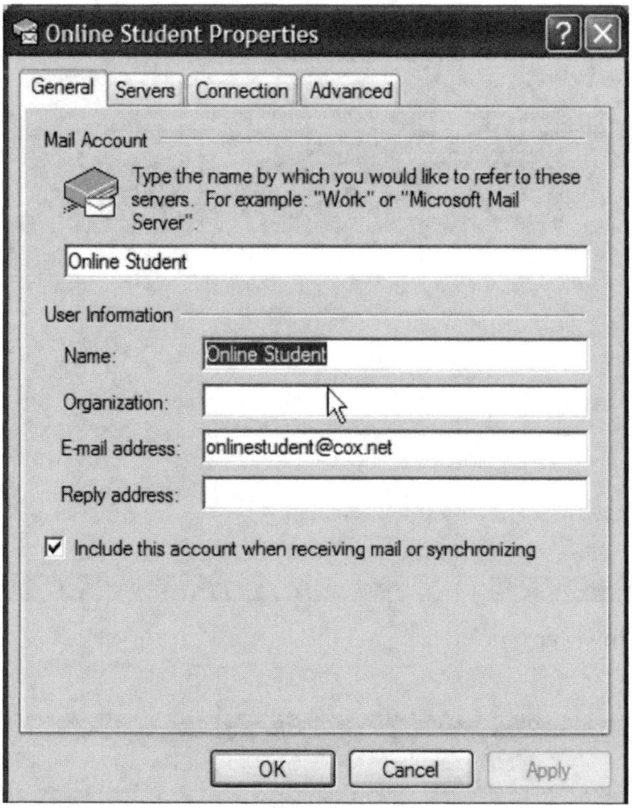

FIGURE 3.3.3 Enter your information in the "Name" field and then click "OK."

FIGURE 3.3.4 Click on "Options."

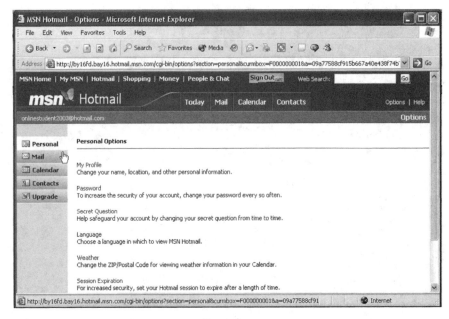

FIGURE 3.3.5 Click on the "Personal" tab.

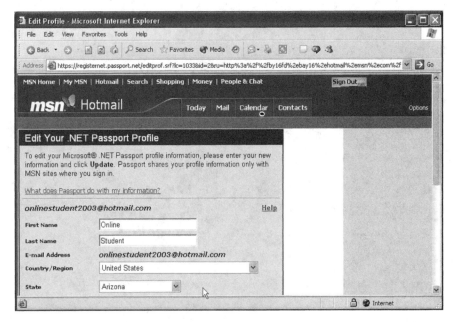

FIGURE 3.3.6 Enter your information.

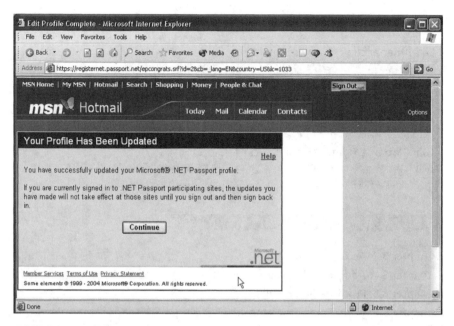

FIGURE 3.3.7 Click "Continue."

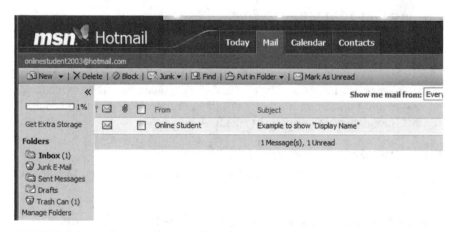

FIGURE 3.3.8 Send yourself an email and notice the "From" field.

OTHER RELEVANT TUTORIALS

Chapter 3.2: Accessing Email
Chapter 3.4: Adding A Signature to Email
Chapter 3.5: Proofreading Email
Chapter 3.6: Using Email Etiquette
Chapter 3.7: Saving Email to Folders
Chapter 3.8: Attaching Files to Email

3.4   Adding a Signature to Email

Introduction

In email, a signature is a block of text that can be added to the end of your email messages. You can set up your email application to add your signature automatically, or you can choose to have it added only when you want to. Your signature should contain your name and email address along with alternative contact information like a phone or fax number.

Online Use of the Competency/Skill

You will know how to create a signature block that can be added to outgoing emails.

Step-by-Step Directions for creating your signature in Microsoft Outlook

Step 1. Go to the "Menu Bar," click on "Tools," and choose "Options" (Figure 3.4.1).

Step 2. Click on the "Preferences" tab and then click on the "Signature Picker . . . " button (Figure 3.4.2).

Step 3. Click on the "New . . . " button (Figure 3.4.3).

Step 4. Enter a name for your signature and then click the "Next" button (Figure 3.4.4).

Step 5. Enter your signature information in the "Signature Text" box and then click the "Finish" button (Figure 3.4.5).

Step 6. Click the "OK" button (Figure 3.4.6).

Step 7. Click the "OK" button (Figure 3.4.7).

Step-by-Step Directions for creating your signature in Hotmail

Step 1. Once you are logged in to your email, click on "Options" (Figure 3.4.8).

Step 2. Click on the "Personal Signature" link (Figure 3.4.9).

Step 3. Type your information in the "Personal Signature" box and then click the "OK" button (Figure 3.4.10).

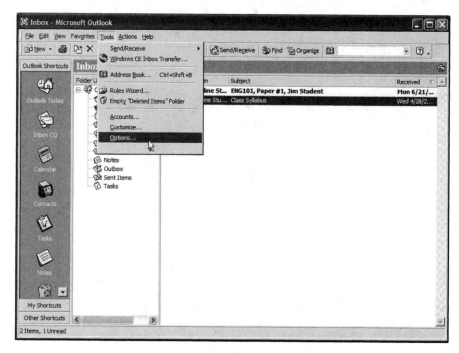

FIGURE 3.4.1 Click on Tools > Options.

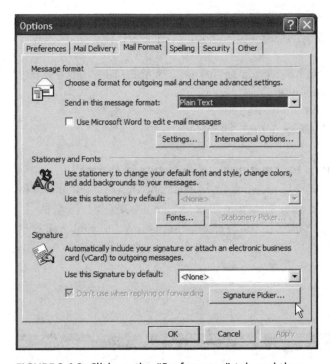

FIGURE 3.4.2 Click on the "Preferences" tab and then click "Signature Picker . . . ."

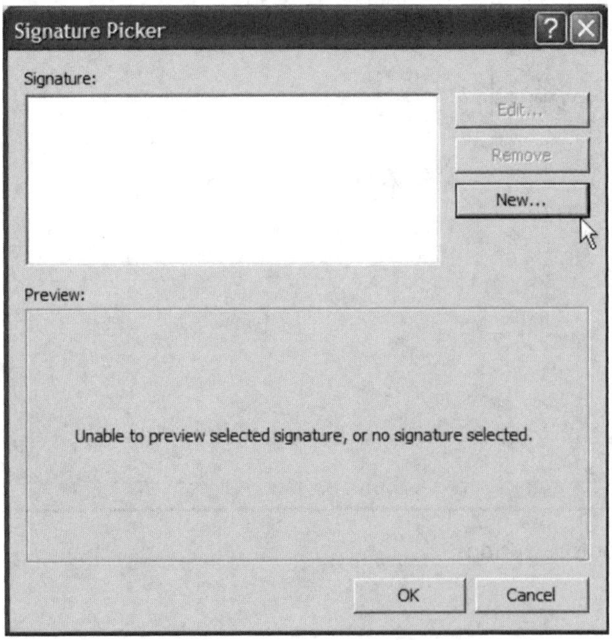

FIGURE 3.4.3 Click "New . . . "

FIGURE 3.4.4 Enter a name for your signature and click "Next."

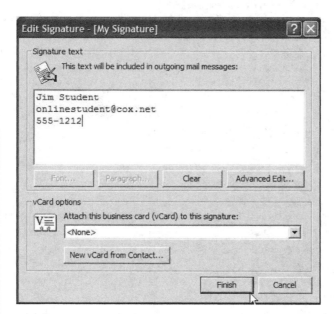

FIGURE 3.4.5 Enter your signature information and click "Finish."

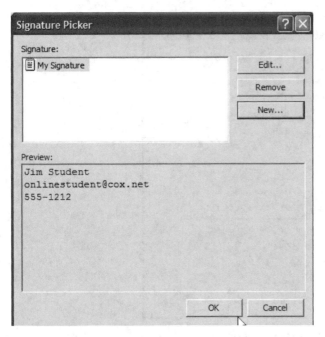

FIGURE 3.4.6 Click "OK."

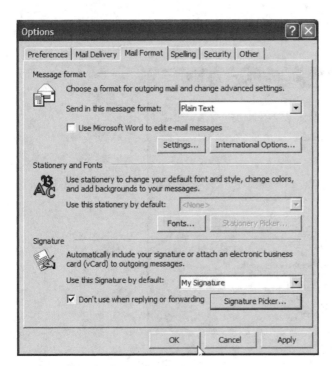

FIGURE 3.4.7 Click "OK."

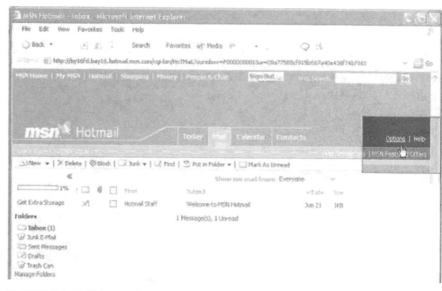

FIGURE 3.4.8 Click "Options."

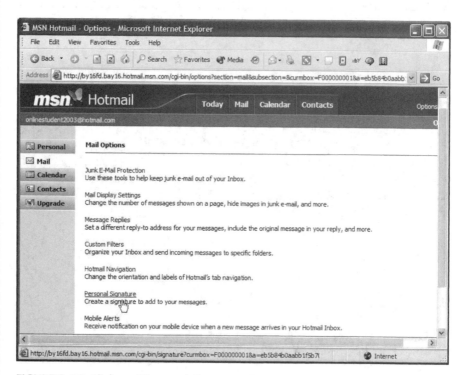

FIGURE 3.4.9 Click on "Personal Signature."

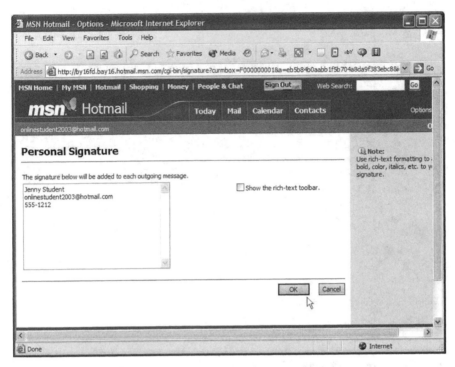

FIGURE 3.4.10 Enter your information and click "OK."

INTERNET RESOURCES

Learnthenet.com, "Harness Email"
http://www.learnthenet.com/english/section/email.html

Web Teacher, "Communication"
http://www.webteacher.org/windows.html

Kaitlin Sherwood's "A Beginner's Guide to Effectively Using Email"
http://www.webfoot.com/advice/email.top.html

GCF Global Learning, "Email Basics"
http://www.gcflearn.org/en/course/course_detail.asp?Course_ID=19&Course_T
itle=Email+Basics

OTHER RELEVANT TUTORIALS

Chapter 3.2: Accessing Email

Chapter 3.3: Identifying the Sender (you) and Subject

3.5   Proofreading Email

Introduction

Before sending an email, make sure your spelling and grammar are correct. Misspellings and poor grammar distract from the subject of the message and reflect poorly on the sender. While most email applications have built-in spelling checkers, most do not have tools to check grammar. If you want to check your grammar before sending your email, copy your message text and paste it into a word processor that has a grammar checker. Once the grammar check is completed, copy and paste the text back into your email message.

Online Use of the Competency/Skill

You will know how to use built-in email spell-checking tools.

Step-by-Step Directions for using the built-in spell checker in Microsoft Outlook

Step 1. Create an email message.

Step 2. Go to the "Menu Bar," click "Tools," and choose "Spelling" (Figure 3.5.1).

Step 3. Choose an appropriate suggestion or action (Figure 3.5.2):

- Click on the "Ignore" button to ignore this instance of the highlighted word.
- Click on the "Ignore All" button to ignore all instances of the highlighted word.
- Click on the "Change" button to use the suggested replacement for this instance of the highlighted word.
- Click on the "Change All" button to use the suggested replacement for all instances of the highlighted word.
- Click on the "Add" button to add the highlighted word to your personal dictionary.

Step 4. The spell checker will continue until the email message is completely checked. Click the "OK" button (Figure 3.5.3).

Step-by-Step Directions for using the built-in spell checker in Hotmail

Step 1. Create an email message.

Step 2. Go to the message "Toolbar," click on "Tools," and choose "Spell Check" (Figure 3.5.4).

Step 3. Choose an appropriate suggestion or action (Figure 3.5.5):

- Click on the "Ignore" button to ignore this instance of the highlighted word.

- Click on the "Ignore All" button to ignore all instances of the highlighted word.
- Click on the "Change Once" button to use the suggested replacement for this instance of the highlighted word.
- Click on the "Change All" button to use the suggested replacement for all instances of the highlighted word.
- Click on the "Add" button to add the highlighted word to your personal dictionary.

Step 4. The spell checker will continue until the email message is completely checked (Figure 3.5.6).

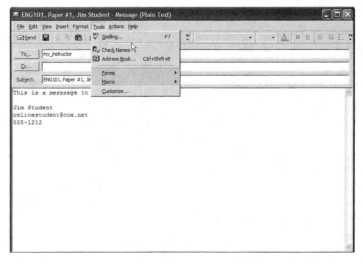

FIGURE 3.5.1 Create an email message and click on Tools > Spelling.

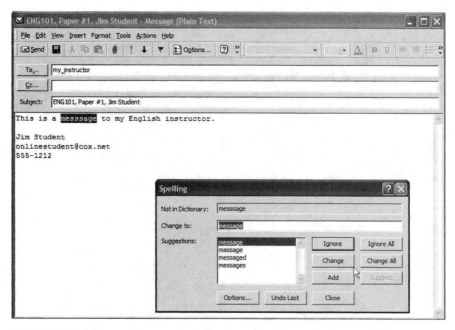

FIGURE 3.5.2 Choose the appropriate suggestion or action.

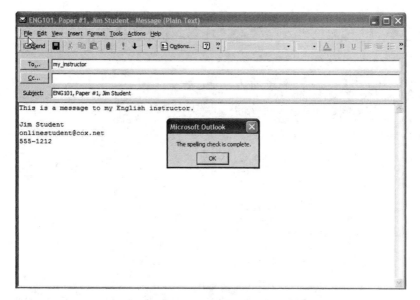

FIGURE 3.5.3 Let the spell checker continue until the message is completely checked, then click "OK."

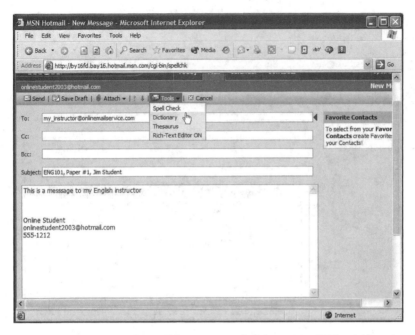

FIGURE 3.5.4 Create an email message and click on "Spell Check."

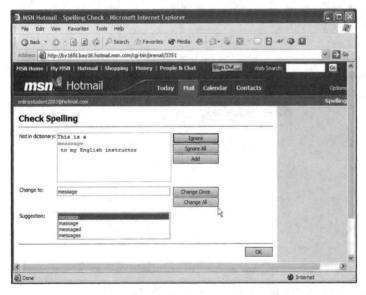

FIGURE 3.5.5 Choose the appropriate suggestion or action.

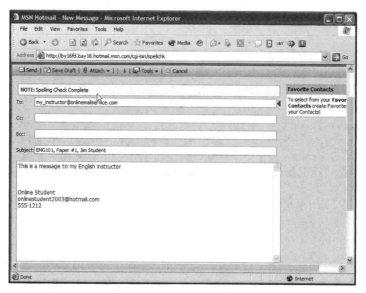

FIGURE 3.5.6 Let the spell checker continue until the message is completely checked.

INTERNET RESOURCES

Learnthenet.com, "Harness Email"
http://www.learnthenet.com/english/section/email.html

Web Teacher, "Communication"
http://www.webteacher.org/windows.html

Kaitlin Sherwood's "A Beginner's Guide to Effectively Using Email"
http://www.webfoot.com/advice/email.top.html

GCF Global Learning, "Email Basics"
http://www.gcflearn.org/en/course/course_detail.asp?Course_ID=19&Course_Title=Email+Basics

OTHER RELEVANT TUTORIALS

Chapter 3.1: Using Email Effectively in Online Courses

Chapter 3.4: Adding a Signature to Email

3.6   Using Email Etiquette

Introduction

Using good email etiquette is important when communicating with instructors, fellow students, and friends. Put some thought into the creation of your message so that it concisely says what you actually want it to say. A rambling email message can waste busy instructors' and fellow students' time. Grammatical and spelling errors distract from the point you are trying to make. You should also make it easy to identify who is sending the message and what it is about. Many think that email is an informal form of communicating, but when it is with instructors and fellow students, it is best to use care when sending email.

Online Use of the Competency/Skill

You will know how to create emails that are well constructed and useful to the recipient.

Step-by-Step Directions

The following are steps to take to create an effective email. These steps do not need to be done in any particular order, but each should be considered.

Step 1. Use Non-Cryptic Addresses and Display Names—By default, many email applications will show your email address as the person an email is from. If you send an email to your instructor and your email address is xyz123@onlinemail provider.com, he or she may not be able to tell who sent it if they are not familiar with your address. It would be more useful if the "From" field had your actual name. Most email applications allow you to modify something called a "Display Name" (or something similar). This display name field is where you can put in your name. While you can type in just about anything, it is best to use your actual name. "Super Student" or other such phrases can be irritating to the recipient and hinder their ability to quickly identify who sent it.

Step 2. Use Informative Subject Lines—You should always include a meaningful subject line in your message. Some useful information for an online student to include might be the class, assignment and student name, e.g. ENG101, Paper #1, Jim Student. Your instructor may have you add something like "***Help***" if you need a quick response. A subject line of "Help on assignment 1" would be pretty much useless. Ask your instructor if he or she has a particular format they would prefer that you use.

If you are reply to an email but wish to change the subject, change the subject line, also. Better yet, create a new email with the new subject. The subject line is usually the easiest way to follow the conversation and for filing, so changing the conversation without changing the subject will be confusing.

Step 3. Consider message length, content, and format. Make your message as long or short as it needs to be. Provide enough information to make your point or ask a question, but stick to the subject and don't ramble on. Don't type your

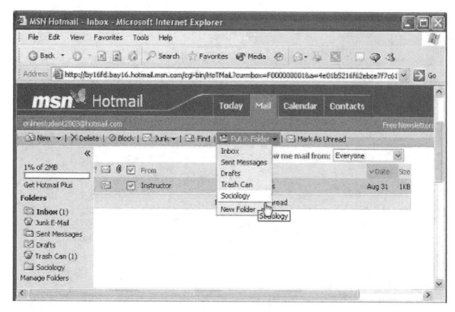

FIGURE 3.7.9 Your new folder appears in the folder list. You can now move emails into the new folder.

INTERNET RESOURCES

Learnthenet.com, "Harness Email"
http://www.learnthenet.com/english/section/email.html

Web Teacher, "Communication"
http://www.webteacher.org/windows.html

Kaitlin Sherwood's "A Beginner's Guide to Effectively Using Email"
http://www.webfoot.com/advice/email.top.html

GCF Global Learning, "Email Basics"
http://www.gcflearn.org/en/course/course_detail.asp?Course_ID=19&Course_T
itle=Email+Basics

OTHER RELEVANT TUTORIALS

Chapter 3.1: Using Email Effectively in Online Courses
Chapter 3.2: Accessing Email
Chapter 3.12: Maintaining Your Email Account

3.8   Attaching Files to Email

Introduction

When you take online courses, you will often complete assignments using word processing applications, spreadsheet programs, or programming tools. You will usually have to send your assignment to your instructor via email as an attachment. You can send email with attachments whether you are using an application such as Microsoft Outlook or an online email service like Hotmail.

Online Use of the Competency/Skill

You will know how to send files as attachments to email.

Step-by-Step Directions for Microsoft Outlook

Step 1. Go to the "Tool Bar" and click on the "New" button (Figure 3.8.1).

Step 2. Fill in the subject line (Figure 3.8.2).

Step 3. Compose the body of the message. Remember to include your full name (Figure 3.8.2).

Step 4. Type in the recipient's address or choose from your address book (Figure 3.8.2).

Step 5. Go to the message "Tool Bar" and click on the "Insert File" button (Figure 3.8.2).

Step 6. Navigate to where your file is saved on your computer (Figure 3.8.3).

Step 7. Highlight the file you want to attach (Figure 3.8.3).

Step 8. Click the "Insert" button (Figure 3.8.3).

Step-by-Step Directions for Hotmail

Step 1. Go to the "Tool Bar" and click on the "New" button (Figure 3.8.4).

Step 2. Fill in the subject line (Figure 3.8.5).

Step 3. Compose the body of the message. Remember to include your full name (Figure 3.8.5).

Step 4. Type in the recipient's address or choose from your address book (Figure 3.8.5).

Step 5. Go to the message "Tool Bar," click on the "Attach" button, and then choose "File" (Figure 3.8.5).

Step 6. Click on the "Browse . . . " button (Figure 3.8.6).

Step 7. Navigate to where your file is saved on your computer (Figure 3.8.7).

Step 8. Click the "Open" button (Figure 3.8.7).

Step 9. Click on the "OK" button or "OK and Attach Another" (Figure 3.8.8).

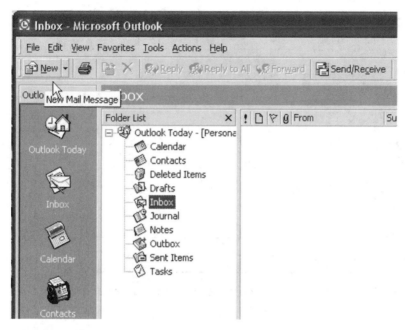

FIGURE 3.8.1 Create a new email message.

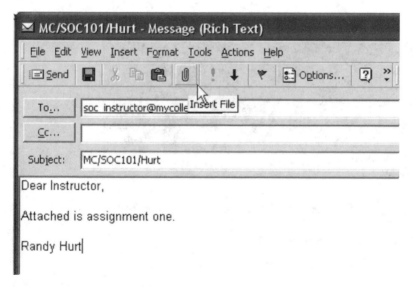

FIGURE 3.8.2 Fill in the necessary information and click on the "Insert File" button.

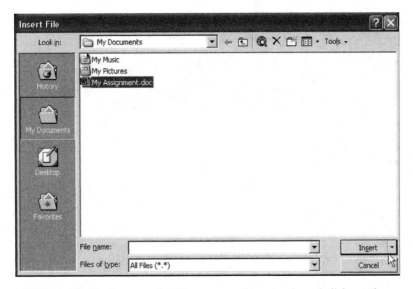

FIGURE 3.8.3 Navigate to the file you want to attach and click on the "Insert" button.

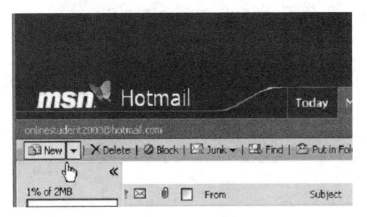

FIGURE 3.8.4 Click on the "New" button.

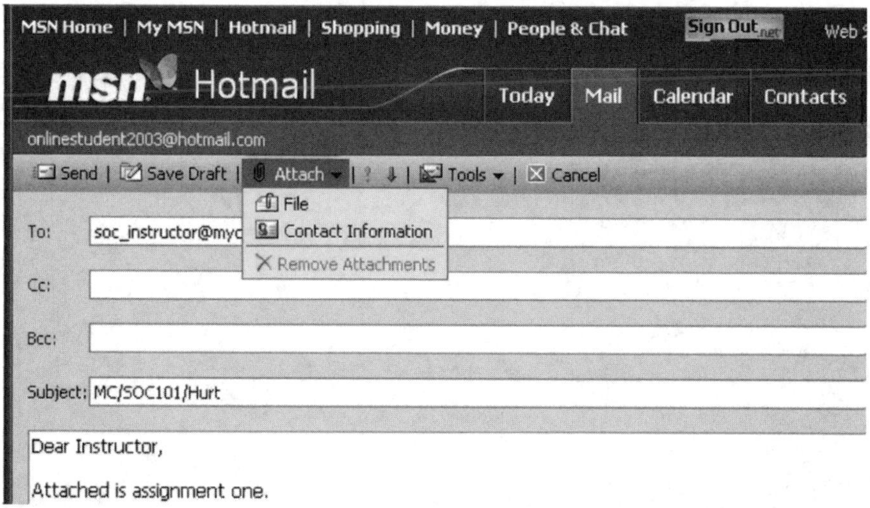

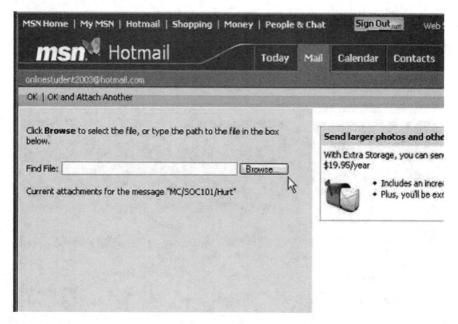

FIGURE 3.8.5 Fill in the necessary information, click on the "Attach" button, then click "File."

FIGURE 3.8.6 Click on the "Browse" button.

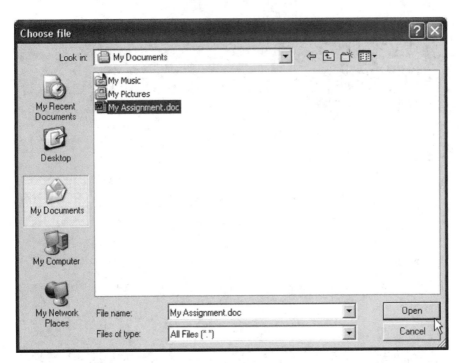

FIGURE 3.8.7 Navigate to the file you want to attach, then click on the "Open" button.

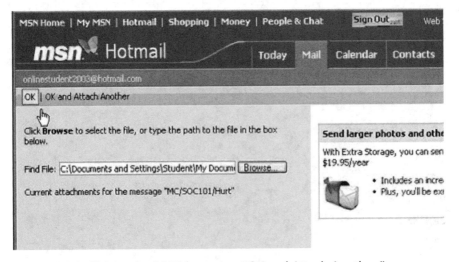

FIGURE 3.8.8 Click on the "OK" button or "OK and Attach Another."

INTERNET RESOURCES

Learnthenet.com, "Harness Email"
http://www.learnthenet.com/english/section/email.html

Web Teacher, "Communication"
http://www.webteacher.org/windows.html

Kaitlin Sherwood's "A Beginner's Guide to Effectively Using Email"
http://www.webfoot.com/advice/email.top.html

GCF Global Learning, "Email Basics"
http://www.gcflearn.org/en/course/course_detail.asp?Course_ID=19&Course_T
itle=Email+Basics

OTHER RELEVANT TUTORIALS

3.9   Protecting Your Computer from Email Viruses

Introduction

Email is one of the most common ways for computer viruses to spread. Computer viruses can cause harmless annoyances like pop-up messages or they can run harmful system-crashing programs. Computer viruses are generally small programs, usually written with malicious intent, that attach themselves to other programs or files. Viruses will often infect programs in a computer and then spread to other computers, infecting them as well. While it is impossible to completely protect your computer from all viruses, there are some precautions you can take to protect your system.

Online Use of the Competency/Skill

You will know how to protect your computer from email viruses.

Step-by-Step Directions

There are several things you can do to help keep your computer secure from email-borne viruses. These need not be in any particular order.

Step 1. Be sure you have anti-virus software loaded on your computer. Have it scan your system periodically, either manually or automatically, and be sure that you have the latest virus definition files from the anti-virus software vendor. Most anti-virus software will allow you to configure it to check for updates automatically.

Step 2. Make sure you have the latest patches and updates for your email application. If you are using an email package such as Microsoft Outlook or Outlook Express, check regularly with the vendor for updates or patches. These updates and patches often have fixes for security holes or vulnerabilities and are usually downloadable from the vendor's website for free.

Step 3. Use caution with attachments. Before opening an attachment to an email, make sure you know what the attachment is. Sometimes a virus will use someone's email application to send itself to recipients in that person's address book and it will look like it came from someone you know. If you get an email with an attachment from someone you know, but you were not expecting an attachment from that person, then contact the person by email or phone and find out what the attachment is before you open it. As a good practice, if you plan to send an attachment to someone, let him or her know, with an email or phone call, to expect it.

INTERNET RESOURCES

Learnthenet.com, "Harness Email"
http://www.learnthenet.com/english/section/email.html

Web Teacher, "Communication"
http://www.webteacher.org/windows.html

Kaitlin Sherwood's "A Beginner's Guide to Effectively Using Email"
http://www.webfoot.com/advice/email.top.html

GCF Global Learning, "Email Basics"
http://www.gcflearn.org/en/course/course_detail.asp?Course_ID=19&Course_T
itle=Email+Basics

OTHER RELEVANT TUTORIALS

Chapter 2.18: Protecting Your Computer from Viruses
Chapter 2.19: Setting Security Measures for Your Computer

3.10   Saving Email to Draft Mode for Review

Introduction

Most of the time you will create an email and send it immediately. There will be times, however, when you decide that you would like to wait to send it. You may find that you need to gather some more information before you send the email, or you might want to have some time for reflection to ensure that what you have written is actually what you want to say. Rather than canceling out and delet-ing the email you have started, you can save it as a draft. When you are ready, you can open the draft email, reread it, and edit it before sending.

Online Use of the Competency/Skill

You will know how to save an email message as a draft.

Step-by-Step Directions for saving an email as a draft in Microsoft Outlook

Step 1. Create a new email message (Figure 3.10.1).

Step 2. Click on the "X" at the top right of the email message window. A dialog box will pop up asking if you would like to save the email. Click "Yes" (Figure 3.10.2).

Step 3. Your email will be saved to the "Drafts" folder (Figure 3.10.3).

Step 4. Click on the email to open the email to edit and send.

Step-by-Step Directions for saving an email as a draft in Hotmail

Step 1. Create an email message (Figure 3.10.4).

Step 2. Click on the "Save Draft" button (Figure 3.10.5).

Step 3. Your email will be saved to the "Drafts" folder (Figure 3.10.6).

Step 4. Click on the email to open the email to edit and send.

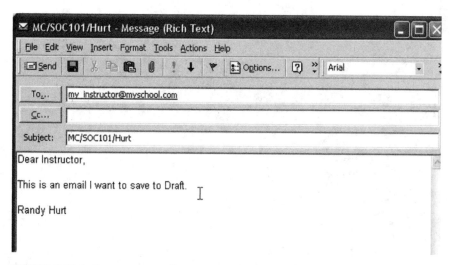

FIGURE 3.10.1 Create an email message.

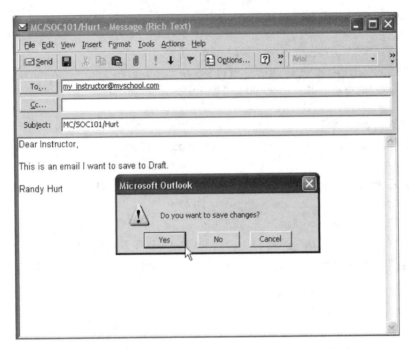

FIGURE 3.10.2 Click on the "X" at the top right of the email message window. Click "Yes" in the dialog box.

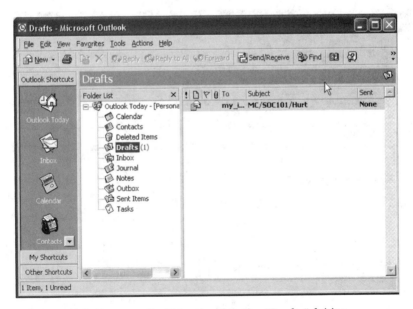

FIGURE 3.10.3 Your email will be saved to the "Drafts" folder.

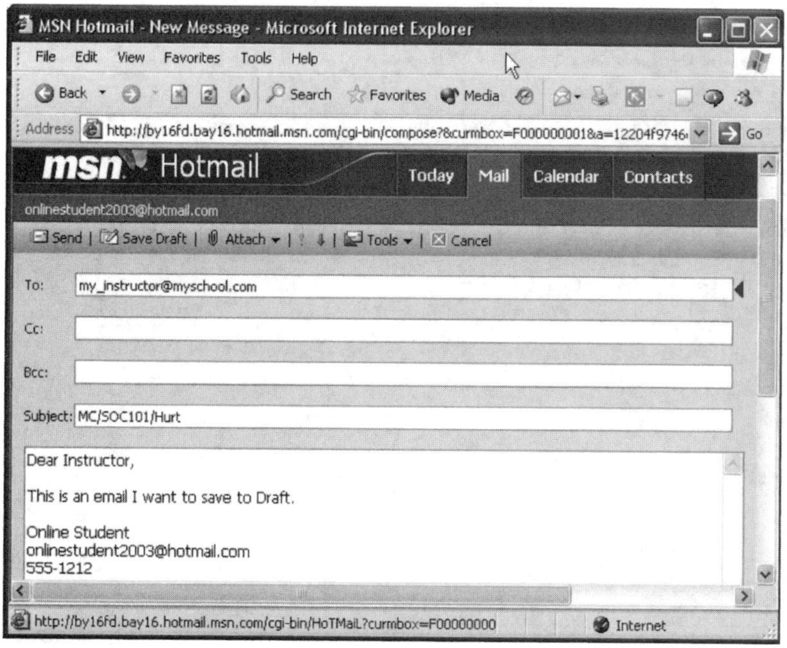

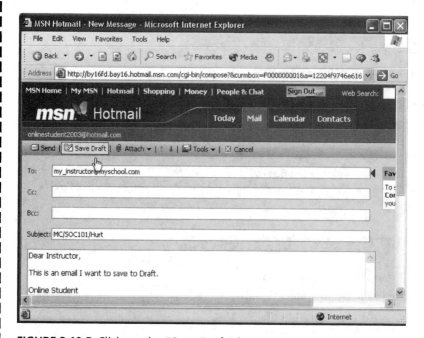

FIGURE 3.10.4 Create an email message.

FIGURE 3.10.5 Click on the "Save Draft" button.

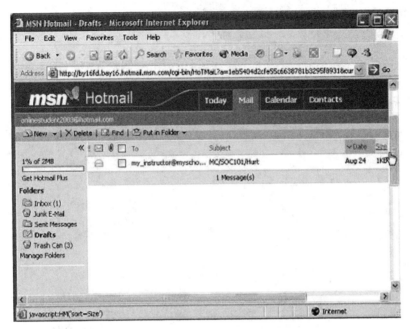

FIGURE 3.10.6 Your email will appear in the "Drafts" folder.

INTERNET RESOURCES

Learnthenet.com, "Harness Email"
http://www.learnthenet.com/english/section/email.html

Web Teacher, "Communication"
http://www.webteacher.org/windows.html

Kaitlin Sherwood's "A Beginner's Guide to Effectively Using Email"
http://www.webfoot.com/advice/email.top.html

GCF Global Learning, "Email Basics"
http://www.gcflearn.org/en/course/course_detail.asp?Course_ID=19&Course_Title=Email+Basics

OTHER RELEVANT TUTORIALS

Chapter 3.5: Proofreading Email
Chapter 3.6: Using Email Etiquette
Chapter 3.7: Saving Email to Folders

3.11   Setting a High Priority Ranking on Email

Introduction

Most often, you will be satisfied that the recipients of your email will read your message the next time they check their email and will respond in a fairly timely manner. But sometimes what you are sending is important and you would like the recipient to read it as soon as possible. Most email applications allow you to "flag" an email as being of high priority. The high priority email will stand out in the recipient's inbox in some way. It will usually have an exclamation point next to it, or the subject text will be highlighted, or it may be a different color. A high priority flag alerts the recipient that the sender considers the message important. It will not affect the way the email is handled through the email system. The high priority email will not be delivered more quickly, and it won't be delivered to email inboxes that are full and can't receive more messages. It won't cause lower priority messages to be deleted or overwritten so that the high priority message can be delivered.

Online Use of the Competency/Skill

You will be able to set a high priority to an email message.

Step-by-Step Directions for setting a high priority to an email in Microsoft Outlook

Step 1. Create a new email message (Figure 3.11.1).

Step 2. Go to the message "Tool Bar" and click on the exclamation point icon (Figure 3.11.2).

Step 3. The exclamation point will appear next to your email (Figure 3.11.3).

Step-by-Step Directions for setting a high priority to an email in Hotmail.

Step 1. Create a new email message (Figure 3.11.4).

Step 2. Go to the message "Tool Bar" and click on the exclamation point icon (Figure 3.11.5).

Step 3. The exclamation point will appear next to your email (Figure 3.11.6).

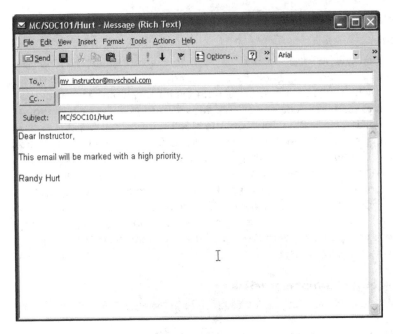

FIGURE 3.11.1 Create an email message.

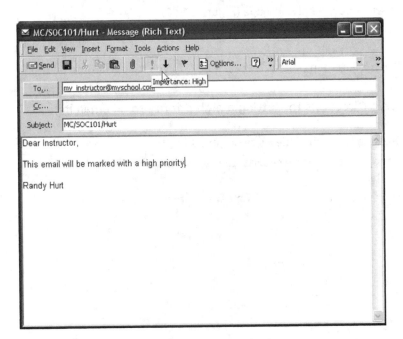

FIGURE 3.11.2 Click on the exclamation point icon.

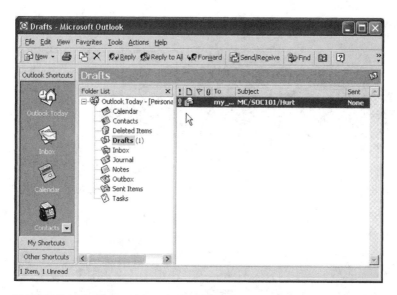

FIGURE 3.11.3 The exclamation point will appear next to your email.

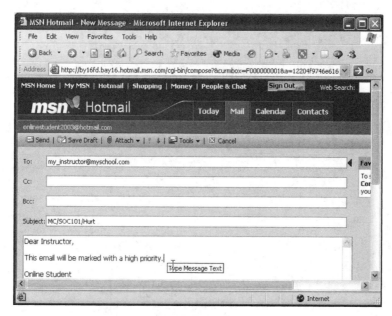

FIGURE 3.11.4 Create an email message.

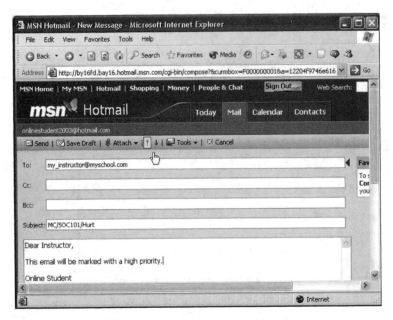

FIGURE 3.11.5 Click on the exclamation point icon.

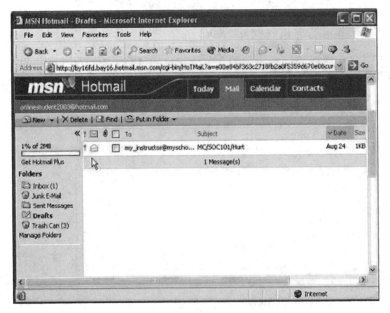

FIGURE 3.11.6 The exclamation point will appear next to your email.

INTERNET RESOURCES

Learnthenet.com, "Harness Email"
http://www.learnthenet.com/english/section/email.html

Web Teacher, "Communication"
http://www.webteacher.org/windows.html

Kaitlin Sherwood's "A Beginner's Guide to Effectively Using Email"
http://www.webfoot.com/advice/email.top.html

GCF Global Learning, "Email Basics"
http://www.gcflearn.org/en/course/course_detail.asp?Course_ID=19&Course_T
itle=Email+Basics

OTHER RELEVANT TUTORIALS

Chapter 3.6: Using Email Etiquette

3.12   Maintaining Your Email Account

Introduction

Most email service providers allow you a maximum amount of hard drive space on their servers for your email. As you use your email, it can be easy to use up this allotted storage space. This is especially the case if you use an online or web-based service such as Hotmail, Yahoo Mail, or email provided by your institution. If you use up this limited storage space, you risk problems like not being able to receive new email because your email provider will reject any incoming email. Even if you use an email application like Microsoft Outlook and have your email service provided by an Internet Service Provider (ISP) like Earthlink, Cox, or another ISP, you can run into storage problems if your application is not configured to store your email locally on your computer. With a few maintenance techniques, you can avoid running into problems with your email account.

Online Use of the Competency/Skill

You will know how to maintain your email account.

Step-by-Step Directions for maintaining your email

Step 1. Clean out old messages from your inbox or other folders you have created. If you have old messages that you no longer need, delete them.

Step 2. Clean out your Sent Items folder. You might be surprised at how many sent messages you have saved that you no longer have any use for.

Step 3. Empty your Deleted Items folder. Most online email services automatically empty Deleted Items folders at some regular interval. In many cases, this folder won't count against your storage space, but you may find some needed space in a hurry.

Step 4. Review and delete, as necessary, any emails from your Draft folder.

Step-by-Step Directions for having your email download to your computer if you use Microsoft Outlook

If you use an email application such as Microsoft Outlook, it is likely that you use email service provided by an ISP. You can avoid using up your storage quota by having your email download from the provider's server to your hard drive.

Step 1. Go to the "Menu Bar," click "Tools," and choose "Accounts . . . " (Figure 3.12.1).

Step 2. Highlight your account under the "Mail" tab in the "Internet Accounts" window and then click the "Properties" button (Figure 3.12.2).

Step 3. Click on the "Advanced" tab (Figure 3.12.3).

Step 4. Under "Delivery," make sure the "Leave a copy of messages on server" checkbox is not checked (Figure 3.12.4).

Step 5. Click the "OK" button in the "Properties" dialog box and then "Close" in the "Internet Accounts" box.

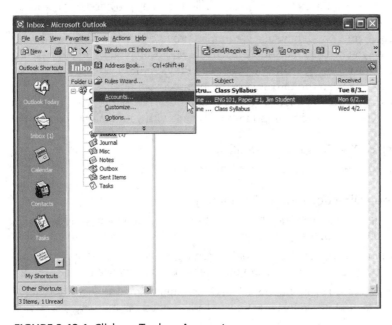

FIGURE 3.12.1 Click on Tools > Accounts.

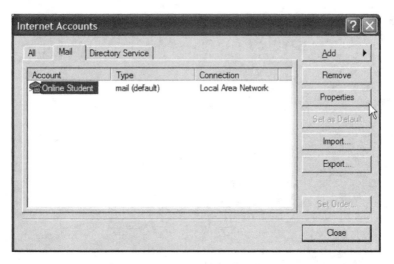

FIGURE 3.12.2 Highlight your account under the "Mail" tab in the "Internet Accounts" window and then click the "Properties" button.

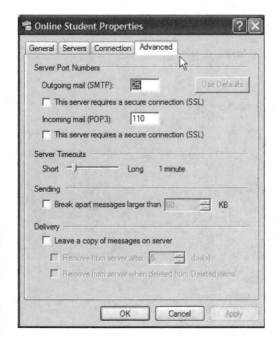

FIGURE 3.12.3 Click on the "Advanced" tab.

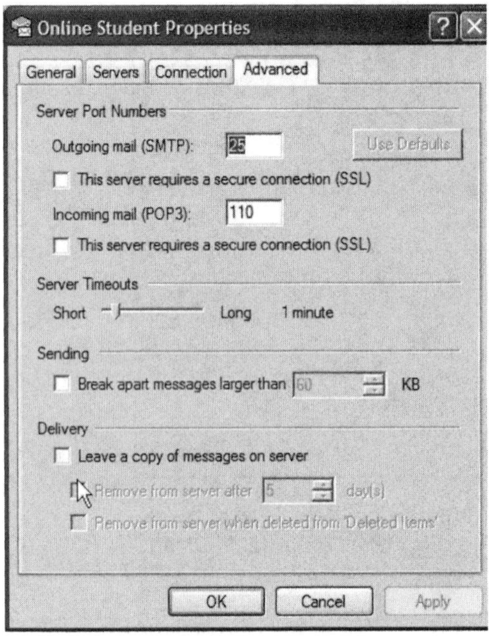

FIGURE 3.12.4 Under "Delivery," make sure the "Leave a copy of messages on server" checkbox is not checked and then click "okay".

INTERNET RESOURCES

Learnthenet.com, "Harness Email"
http://www.learnthenet.com/english/section/email.html

Web Teacher, "Communication"
http://www.webteacher.org/windows.html

Kaitlin Sherwood's "A Beginner's Guide to Effectively Using Email"
http://www.webfoot.com/advice/email.top.html

GCF Global Learning, "Email Basics"
http://www.gcflearn.org/en/course/course_detail.asp?Course_ID=19&Course_Title=Email+Basics

OTHER RELEVANT TUTORIALS

Chapter 3.1: Using Email Effectively in Online Courses

Chapter 3.7: Saving Email to Folders

Chapter 3.9: Protecting Your Computer from Email Viruses

CHAPTER 4

Online Course Tasks for Online Learning

Introduction

Chapter 4 focuses on skills, competencies, and resources that you will use within your online course. The chapter will familiarize you with the online course environment and courseware tools that will make your online learning experience pleasurable and successful. Step-by-step tutorials will help you navigate and master your online course environment. You will become familiar with how your online course functions and how you maneuver and participate within the online course. The step-by-step tutorials in this chapter include accessing, overviewing, navigating, and saving course materials. In addition you will learn how to use the course syllabus, discussion boards, and live chats. You will also become familiar with courseware special tools and help. Mastering these tutorials will ensure your ability to maneuver through your online course with effectiveness, assuring your success.

4.1 Accessing Your Course Anytime, Anywhere

Introduction

The unique phenomenon of online learning is that it connects the disconnected. The online learning environment connects students and instructor via the Internet. Some students may live in the same geographical area of the college, while other students may be located across the state, country, or even in Timbuktu (Mali, Africa). You are able to access your course anytime, anywhere, as long as you have a computer with a modem (phone line, cable, satellite, or wireless). Course access is critical for students who travel frequently, making this unique aspect of online education invaluable. Online learning is truly anywhere, anytime learning.

To access an online course, a computer should meet the following minimum specifications:

- Internet connection.
- Email access.

- Required software: Netscape Communicator/Navigator 6.0 or higher, or Microsoft Internet Explorer 6.0 or higher, or any equivalent web browser.
- Suggested software: Microsoft Office 2000 or XP and Adobe Acrobat Reader.
- Minimum 28.8 KB modem; 56 KB modem recommended.
- 850 MHz or higher processor.
- Minimum 64 MB RAM; 256 MB RAM recommended.
- Monitor capable of at least 800x600 resolution.

Contact your institution concerning specific software or hardware that may be required for your course.

Online Use of the Competency/Skill

You will know how to access your course anytime, even when away from your home computer.

Step-by-Step Directions

Step 1. When you sign up for an online course, here are some immediate things to do:

- Save the URL for your college in your Bookmarks or Favorites in a folder labeled with your college's name.
- Save the URL for your college's Online or Distance Education Campus and save to your college folder.
- Save your online course URL or access URL and save to your college folder.
- Write down and save in a few places your username and password, which allow you to access your online course.

Step 2. Open up a word document and type in all the information you saved in Step 1.

- Save as a file with your college's name and course number. Example: Cochise College SOC101 Notes
- Save to a diskette, CD-R, or flash drive. Label with your institution's name and course number.
- Copy the same file to a folder on your hard drive.

Step 3. Think through what you might need to access your course and to do your coursework when away from your home computer. Add to your diskette any files—course syllabus, important contacts (names, phone numbers, email addresses), and any current projects, assignments, or papers—which will help while you are away from your home computer.

Step 4. Purchase a simple notebook folder with pockets or a three-ring binder. Label with your college's name and course number and title. Insert all important printed course materials and your course diskette.

Step 5. When you travel, pack the above and your textbook or other essential course reading materials.

Step 6. If you travel with a laptop computer, ensure you have a national Internet provider with a local phone number for your destination or a toll-free number. Also, remember to bring all the necessary accessories to make your laptop computer functional.

Step 7. As long as you have your course folder and diskette, you can access your course from a computer at hotel business centers, Kinko's, Internet cafes, libraries, or any computer with a modem.

INTERNET RESOURCES

Delaware Woman Online, "Anytime/Anywhere Learning"
http://www.delawarewoman.com/200204/anytimeany.html

Learning in the New Economy, "Anywhere, Anytime, Take-it-to-go Learning"
http://www.linezine.com/3.1/features/cwdfmw.htm

Learnthenet.com, "Online Learning"
http://www.learnthenet.com/english/html/83online.htm

OTHER RELEVANT TUTORIALS

Chapter 2.4: Accessing Web Pages
Chapter 2.5: Bookmarking Websites and Pages
Chapter 4.2: Saving Course Access Information
Chapter 5.1: Creating a Course Binder for Offline Studying

4.2 Saving Course Access Information

Introduction

The ability to access your online course is crucial. It is also important to be able to access your course at anytime, in any situation, from any place. The excuse that your computer crashed is not acceptable. Your course is accessible anywhere and anytime. Be prepared for any situation and all possibilities.

Online Use of the Competency/Skill

You will ensure access to your course information at all times, in all situations and places.

Step-by-Step Directions

Step 1. Create a document file to write down all information you need to access your online course. Do not trust your memory. Gather and write down the following essentials:

- College homepage URL (web address).
- URL for your course.
- Your user name.
- Your password.
- Any other important URLs: library, learning support center, registration office, and any other online student help resource.

Step 2. Save the information as a file to your hard drive and on a secondary device (diskette, CD-R, or flash drive).

Step 3. Add these important URLs to your Favorites or Bookmarks in a special folder for your college and/or course.

Step 4. Print out all this pertinent information so you can have it as a hard copy and put it into the course binder or folder you have created.

Step 5. Carry this information with you at all times so you can stay connected.

INTERNET RESOURCES

GCF Global Learning, "Internet Lessons"
http://www.gcflearn.org/gcf_classes/internet/index.asp
University of South Dakota Trio Tutorials, "Saving Your Files"
http://www.usd.edu/trio/tut/saving/index.html
Duke University School of Nursing Tutorials, "Managing Your Files"
http://www.duke.edu/~dhewitt/tutorials/explorer/explor.html

OTHER RELEVANT TUTORIALS

Chapter 2.4: Accessing Web Pages
Chapter 2.5: Bookmarking Websites and Pages
Chapter 2.14: Saving Files
Chapter 4.1: Accessing Your Course Anytime, Anywhere
Chapter 5.1: Creating a Course Binder for Offline Studying
Chapter 6.5: Getting Help with Course Problems

4.3   Navigating Online Course Materials

Introduction

Learning what is available in your online course is vital to your success. Take the time to learn all the functions and possibilities of all tabs, bars, icons, and buttons. Learn how to maneuver through the course with efficiency and purpose. Plan on devoting extra time to thoroughly learning the courseware.

Online Use of the Competency/Skill
You will understand all the functions, possibilities, and tools of your online course.

Step-by-Step Directions
Step 1. Access your course and begin to familiarize yourself with the courseware by exploring all tabs, bars, icons, and buttons to discover their function and content.

Step 2. Attend an online student orientation if your institution offers one, or ask if there is an online orientation to the courseware.

Step 3. Take the time to learn the functions of all tabs, bars, buttons, and icons.

Step 4. Remember to refer to the Help button in the courseware to strengthen your familiarization with all contents, functions, and operations of the courseware.

Step 5. See the Internet Resources below if your institution does not provide an orientation.

INTERNET RESOURCES

Washington Online, "An Example of Online Course Navigation"
http://www.waol.org/learnToLearn/Module1/mod1_01.htm

Blackboard Navigation
http://academic.scranton.edu/department/ctle/tutorials/technology/blackboard-NAV

Florida Metropolitan University, "An Example of eCollege Course Navigation"
http://www.fmuonline.com/pdf/handbook.pdf

OTHER RELEVANT TUTORIALS

Chapter 4.14: Using Courseware Special Tools and Resources
Chapter 4.15: Using Courseware Help or Student Help Manual
Chapter 6.5: Getting Help with Course Problems

4.4 Overviewing Course Materials

Introduction
As you begin a new online course, read through the essential course components—syllabus, weekly lessons, materials, assignments, and requirements. Many types of courseware will have specific tabs or buttons that will point you to relevant course materials, such as Announcements, Course Information, Instructor Infor-

mation, Course Documents, Course Assignments, Textbooks, Discussion Board, External Links, and Tools. It is important to take the time to overview and read what your instructor has put into the course. Read thoroughly!

Online Use of the Competency/Skill

You will understand all components of the course and how the course operates.

Step-by-Step Directions

Step 1. Access your course and explore the essential elements of the course—syllabus, assignments, and requirements. Read over these to get a general understanding of the course.

Step 2. Print out all the pertinent course information that you might have to refer to often. Put the information in your course folder or binder.

Step 3. Calendar all your important dates for assignments, papers, live chats, and other elements.

Step 4. Ensure you have a clear understanding of your instructor's expectations and requirements. Especially, read the syllabus thoroughly. Email your instructor for any clarification.

Step 5. Go forth with great confidence and pursue your online course.

INTERNET RESOURCES

Boise State University, "Overview of Blackboard"
http://itc.boisestate.edu/orient/overview.htm
University of Medicine and Dentistry of New Jersey, "Overview of WebCT"
http://www.umdnj.edu/webctweb/basics/
Bunker Hill Community College, "Overview of eCollege"
http://www.bhcc.mass.edu/eCollege/Demos/DemoWebCourse.

OTHER RELEVANT TUTORIALS

Chapter 4.3: Navigating Online Course Materials
Chapter 4.6: Using the Course Syllabus
Chapter 4.14: Using Courseware Special Tools and Resources
Chapter 4.15: Using Courseware Help or Student Help Manual
Chapter 5.2: Overviewing Screen Documents
Chapter 6.15: Following Directions

4.5 Printing Important Course Materials

Introduction

As an online student, you will be spending a lot of time online. To give yourself and your eyes a break, print out all the essential course components—syllabus, weekly lessons, materials, assignments, and requirements. Print out all other information that will be important for offline study, including instructor and college contact information. Put all these printed materials into your course folder or binder and organize it to effectively help you as an offline resource.

Online Use of the Competency/Skill

You will have print copies of pertinent documents for offline access.

Step-by-Step Directions

Step 1. Access your online course.

Step 2. Navigate to the sections of the course that will be essential to print for offline referral, review, and study.

Step 3. Print each web page or document. You can use different printing options to capture the materials:

- Printer icon from your browser.
- From "File" choose "Print."
- On your keyboard, press CTRL + P.
- On web pages, do a mouse right-click.

Step 4. Store and organize materials in your course folder.

INTERNET RESOURCES

Printing Course Documents
http://alto.aber.al.uk/bb/helpsheets/student_print.asp
GCF Global Learning
http://www.gcflearn.org/en/main/students.asp

OTHER RELEVANT TUTORIALS

Chapter 4.4: Overviewing Course Materials
Chapter 5.1: Creating a Course Binder for Offline Studying
Chapter 6.3: Getting Help with Computer Problems

4.6   Using the Course Syllabus

Introduction

The course syllabus is the heart and soul of your course. The syllabus will give you a snapshot, guide, and map for what the course will entail. Some of the major components of a good syllabus are basic course information which includes pre-requisites, course overview, objectives, textbooks and any additional materials, assignments with due dates, grading and other course policies, and other instructor expectations. A comprehensive syllabus provides the best possible description of course expectations and activities. Use the syllabus to help you navigate the course with less confusion or ambiguity.

Online Use of the Competency/Skill

You will understand the course syllabus and use it as a viable working tool for the duration of the course.

Step-by-Step Directions

Step 1. Access your online course and locate the course syllabus or course information.

Step 2. Print the information and add to your course folder or binder for offline reference.

Step 3. Read thoroughly, highlight important information, and make notes.

Step 4. Calendar all assignment due dates and any other significant course dates.

Step 5. Review the course syllabus periodically.

Step 6. Email your instructor if you have any questions or need clarification.

INTERNET RESOURCES

"Succeeding in Distance Education Courses"
http://www.studygs.net/distanceed.htm

Cleveland State University, "Course Syllabus"
http://www.csuohio.edu/gradcollege/student/handbook/chapters/syllabus.htm

Mansfield University Center for Effective Teaching, "Getting On the Syllabus"
http://www.mnsfld.edu/~effteach/99decAcronym.html

OTHER RELEVANT TUTORIALS

Chapter 4.3: Navigating Online Course Materials
Chapter 4.4: Overviewing Course Materials
Chapter 5.1: Creating a Course Binder for Offline Studying
Chapter 6.5: Getting Help with Course Problems
Chapter 6.15: Following Directions

4.7   Participating in Discussion Boards

Introduction

The course discussion board is an asynchronous tool used to communicate with your instructor and fellow students. Take the time to familiarize yourself with the discussion board and learn how it operates. Discussion boards offer a great way to post messages and engage in discussions that are instructor led. Participating in discussion boards can greatly enhance your course experience. In the discussion boards, you can not only learn from the ideas and thoughts of others, but also contribute some of your own. Be aware that some online courses will require your participation in the discussion boards as a percentage of your grade. Your participation and interactivity in the discussion boards may be graded for quantity and quality.

Online Use of the Competency/Skill

You will know how to participate effectively in discussion boards.

Step-by-Step Directions

Step 1. Access your course and click on the appropriate button that will lead you to the discussion boards.

Step 2. Select the appropriate discussion topic or discussion forum to participate in. Most discussion board topics will be listed by the course week or lesson.

Step 3. Select the specific discussion you want to post or reply to.

Step 4. Read the posted topic thoroughly before replying. A discussion topic may require some reading and research.

Step 5. Write your response in a document and use the software tools to check grammar, punctuation, and spelling.

Step 6. Copy and paste your response into the reply box.

Step 7. Preview your response and then submit it.

INTERNET RESOURCES

Washtenaw Community College, "Participating in Discussion Boards"
http://www.wccnet.edu/resources/computerresources/blackboard/pdf/
Discussion_Boards.pdf

OTHER RELEVANT TUTORIALS

Chapter 4.8: Netiquette in Discussion Boards
Chapter 4.9: Creating a New Thread/Topic in Discussion Boards
Chapter 4.10: Replying in Discussion Boards
Chapter 5.8: Editing and Proofing Your Writing
Chapter 5.9: Writing Responses to Assigned Questions on Course Reading

4.8   Netiquette in Discussion Boards

Introduction

Posting in discussion boards requires forethought, courtesy, and politeness. Polite behavior helps to create a comfortable learning environment where online interactivity and community building take place. Maintain a professional behavior as you communicate with others. Remember your communication in discussion boards is a reflection of you. Develop the skills to communicate effectively in the online environment.

Online Use of the Competency/Skill

You will know the netiquette to use in discussion boards.

Step-by-Step Directions

Step 1. Take the time to review the thread or discussion you are replying to. Stay on task, and target the initial topic posted by the instructor.

Step 2. Be careful how you express emotion and humor in the discussion boards.

Step 3. Refrain from online acronyms and emoticons and other communication shortcuts. Strive to communicate clearly and succinctly.

Step 4. Discuss course issues and topics via the discussion boards. Use email or phone to communicate personal issues or dialogue one on one.

Step 5. Work up your response in a document so you can check grammar, punctuation, and spelling. Be a professional student.

Step 6. Review your response before submitting it to ensure you are communicating effectively and with courtesy.

Step 7. Be diligent in helping to create a positive learning environment and community of online learners.

INTERNET RESOURCES

Netiquette, "Netiquette for Discussion Groups"
http://www.albion.com/netiquette/book/0963702513p65.html

Online Netiquette, "Netiquette Matters"
http://www.onlinenetiquette.com/netiquette_guide.html

Netiquette Now, "Netiquette for Newsgroups, Bulletin Boards and Discussion"
http://www.advicemeant.com/netiquet/usenet.shtml

OTHER RELEVANT TUTORIALS

Chapter 4.7: Participating in Discussion Boards
Chapter 4.9: Creating a New Thread/Topic in Discussion Boards
Chapter 4.10: Replying in Discussion Boards
Chapter 6.10: Getting Along with Your Instructor
Chapter 6.11: Getting Along with Your Fellow Students

4.9 Creating a New Thread/Topic in Discussion Boards

Introduction

Discussion boards are a vital component of the online course for great communication exchange and online community building. Discussion boards contain messages that are usually organized by "threads" or special topic areas. Threads are topics created and posted by your instructor to stimulate discussion on that topic. The thread keeps everyone focused on that topic by posting messages at the same place to the same thread. Some instructors will develop the course with discussion boards that are reply-only threads. Some courses will allow you to post new threads or topics in the discussion boards. Always be specific, and target the focus of the topic. Most importantly, always ensure that you are replying to the person you truly want to reply to by maintaining good and accurate threading.

Online Use of the Competency/Skill

You will know how to post a new thread in a discussion board and to follow a threaded topic with continuity.

Step-by-Step Directions

Step 1. Access your course, and click on the button that will lead you to the discussion board.

Step 2. Select the appropriate discussion board.

Step 3. To add or start a thread, click on the "Add New Thread" button at the top of the screen.

Step 4. Work up your response in a document so you can check grammar, punctuation, and spelling. Create a good subject header.

Step 5. Review your new thread before submitting it to ensure you are communicating effectively.

Step 6. Copy and paste your new thread into the box and type an appropriate subject header.

Step 7. Preview your response and then submit it.

INTERNET RESOURCES

University of Texas, "Using the Discussion Board"
http://www.utexas.edu/academic/blackboard/tutorials/pdfs/Discussion.pdf

Washtenaw Community College, "Participating in Discussion Boards"
http://www.wccnet.edu/resources/computerresources/blackboard/pdf/
Discussion_Boards.pdf

OTHER RELEVANT TUTORIALS

Chapter 4.7: Participating in Discussion Boards
Chapter 4.8: Netiquette in Discussion Boards
Chapter 4.10: Replying in Discussion Boards
Chapter 5.9: Writing Responses to Assigned Questions on Course Reading

4.10   Replying in Discussion Boards

Introduction

Discussion boards are asynchronous threaded messages that allow you the flexibility and convenience to participate by replying to your instructor and fellow students. Most coursework occurs in discussion boards where you will reply to threads initiated by your instructor. It is very important that you take the time to master how to post your responses correctly. In some courses you will be graded on the quantity and quality of your replies to the instructor and fellow students. Read your assignments ahead of time, and then take the time to craft meaningful and intelligent responses.

Online Use of the Competency/Skill

You will know how to reply effectively to topic threads in discussion boards.

Step-by-Step Directions

Step 1. Access your course, and click on the button that will lead you to the discussion board.

Step 2. Select the appropriate discussion topic or discussion forum to participate in. Most discussion board topics will be listed by the course week or lesson.

Step 3. Select the specific discussion you want to reply to.

Step 4. Read the posted topic thoroughly before replying. Some discussion topics will require some reading and research. Work up your response in a document so you can check grammar, punctuation, and spelling.

Step 5. Click on the reply button. Copy and paste your response into the reply box.

Step 6. Preview your response and then submit it.

Step 7. Your posted reply will now be a part of the discussion board thread.

INTERNET RESOURCES

Washtenaw Community College, "Participating in Discussion Boards"
http://www.wccnet.edu/resources/computerresources/blackboard/pdf/
Discussion_Boards.pdf

University of Texas, "Using the Discussion Board"
http://www.utexas.edu/academic/blackboard/tutorials/pdfs/Discussion.pdf

4.11   Submitting Assignments

Introduction

Completing assignments in a timely and thorough manner will affect your final grade. Devote time to understanding the directions and guidance for each assignment. Do most of your study and work offline in a document so you can take the time for quality work. Adhere to all guidance and directions given by your instructor. Be timely and submit work on or before due dates. Submitting work in the correct way and place is very important. Many online courses will allow multiple ways to submit work. Online assignments can be posted in many ways:

- Email attachment.
- Discussion board.
- Digital drop box.
- Assignment file upload.
- Course portfolio.

   Follow the directions outlined in your course syllabus and the specific guidance of your instructor for submitting all assignments.

Online Use of the Competency/Skill

You will know how to post required assignments on time and in the correct way or place.

Step-by-Step Directions

Step 1. Read the requirements for each assignment and prepare your work in a document. Label your assignment by including the assignment title, your full name, the course number, and the date of submission.

Step 2. Review and proofread your assignment prior to submitting it.

Step 3. Always save your work!! Create a course folder and save all your digital files for the course. Keeping a copy of your submitted assignments is your best safeguard against delays and extra work.

Step 4. Submit your assignment in the correct format and procedure.

Step 5. Double check that your assignment was submitted successfully:

- Save all your "Sent" email for the course to your course email folder.
- Inside your online course, refresh the screen to see that your assignment was posted to the appropriate place—discussion board, digital drop box, assignment file uploads, or other location.

Step 6. Check your online course gradebook about a week to 10 days after submittal. If a grade is not posted, ask your instructor.

INTERNET RESOURCES

University of Texas Distance Education Center, "Guidance for Submitting Assignments"
http://www.dec.utexas.edu/onlinecourses/submitassign.html
Dakota County Technical College, "Example of Submitting Assignments in WebCT"
http://www.dctc.mnscu.edu/olc/assign.html
UCLA Extension, "Example of Submitting Assignments in Blackboard"
http://www.victoriawebpages.com/viewlets/assess/assess_viewlet.html

OTHER RELEVANT TUTORIALS

Chapter 2.14: Saving Files
Chapter 3.8: Attaching Files to Email
Chapter 5.5: Completing Online Course Assignments
Chapter 6.5: Getting Help with Course Problems
Chapter 6.8: Managing Time for Online Learning
Chapter 6.15: Following Directions

4.12 Accessing and Participating in a Live Chat

Introduction

Live chats offer a great opportunity for on time questions, course dialogue, and online course community building. Live chats help to create a sense of connectedness and thus help to connect the geographically disconnected through the online course. One of the most exciting things about online courses is the ability to have synchronous conversations with your instructor and fellow students using a live chat function. Live chats allow for synchronous meetings, meaning that everyone gathers at their computer at a definitive time so conversations are occurring in "real" time with all participants in the chat room at the same time. Be aware that some instructors will have mandatory live chats and you will be graded for your participation and interactivity.

Online Use of the Competency/Skill

You will know how to access and participate in a live chat.

Step-by-Step Directions

Step 1. Access your online course, and click on the communication button or icon.

Step 2. Select "Live Chat." If this is the first time you accessed the live chat tool or feature, you may get a message to download chat software. The download will take a few minutes.

Step 3. Take the time to familiarize yourself with the features and icons of the live chat tool.

Step 4. Sign on 10 minutes prior to the live chat to ensure access and that all software is functioning well.

Step 5. Read and follow the live chat discussion. Live chats move quickly. Adhere to any instructor guidance.

Step 6. Watch your spelling, punctuation, and grammar as you post. Be thoughtful and courteous.

Step 7. Submit your contributions.

INTERNET RESOURCES

Case Western Reserve University, "Blackboard Communication Tools"
http://www.cwru.edu/net/csg/CI/virchat.html

Oregon State University, "Blackboard Virtual Classroom"
http://oregonstate.edu/instruct/coursedev/tutorials/Bb/virtual_classroom.htm

Palm Beach Community College, "WebCT Communication"
http://www.pbcc.edu/faculty/ottp/WebCT_site/7_Communication/7communemenu.htm

OTHER RELEVANT TUTORIALS

Chapter 4.8: Netiquette in Discussion Boards
Chapter 4.13: Communicating Effectively in a Live Chat
Chapter 6.10: Getting Along with Your Instructor
Chapter 6.11: Getting Along with Your Fellow Students
Chapter 6.15: Following Directions

4.13 Communicating Effectively in a Live Chat

Introduction

Live chats in the online environment basically have two purposes: building community and connectedness, and adding a personal dimension to course content. Live chats have greater value when led by an instructor who keeps the students on task with the course content. If you wish to chitchat with one or more students, the live chat in a course is not the place. Use email or phone to do so. Be proactive and up-to-date on your assignment, reading prior to the live chat. To communicate effectively requires forethought, timeliness, staying on topic, and being courteous. Help to create an ongoing positive live chat learning environment.

Online Use of the Competency/Skill

You will be able to effectively communicate in a live chat.

Step-by-Step Directions

Step 1. Prepare for your live chat by reading scheduled assignments. Open up a document and write questions and some generic statements pertaining to the scheduled chat so that all you have to do is copy and paste your writing into the live chat box.

Step 2. Access your online course, click on the communication icon, and select "Live Chat."

Step 3. Adhere to any instructor guidance and the basic rules of netiquette by being thoughtful and courteous.

Step 4. Use correct spelling, punctuation, and grammar.

Step 5. Submit your contributions and continue to follow the flow of the discussion.

INTERNET RESOURCES

Homepage Made Easy, "Communicating Online"
http://www.homepagemadeeasy.com/communicate4.html

University of Wisconsin–Madison, "Communicating in an Online Environment"
http://wiscinfo.doit.wisc.edu/ltde/ORFI/ces/print/communicating.htm

Mentor Place, "Common Issues in Online Communication"
http://www.mentorplace.org/MPT/MPTCCommonIssues.htm

4.14   Using Courseware Special Tools and Resources

Introduction

Your courseware management system (Blackboard, WebCT, eCollege, or other system) contains many tools and resources that will help you succeed as an online student. You need to know how to access and use special tools within the online course such as gradebook, personal profile, calendar, external web links, and others. Some of these additional tools will help you in completing your assignments, communicating, and tracking your grades and progress in the course. Many online courses have a variety of assessments: quizzes, exams, and surveys, for example. It is important that you learn how to access your course assessments and take them effectively and efficiently. Your first online course will require extra time and energy to learn all of the special tools and resources provided in the courseware. Doing so will be very worthwhile in your pursuit to get an A for your course and to be the very best online student you can be.

Online Use of the Competency/Skill

You will understand the special tools and other resources within the online course.

Step-by-Step Directions

Step 1. Access your online course, and review all buttons, tabs, and icons.

Step 2. Familiarize yourself with all the additional tools and resources by clicking around and investigating all areas of your course. The invested time will prove worthwhile, especially as you begin to take other online courses.

Step 3. Experiment with some of the tools and resources to see how they work.

Step 4. Find the student Help manual that goes with the courseware. Read and learn how some of the additional tools and resources can help you pursue the course requirements and help you be a successful online student.

Step 5. Contact your institution's Help Desk for any other help or guidance with the tools and resources that make up your online course.

INTERNET RESOURCES

Ball State University, "Blackboard Tutorials"
http://web.bsu.edu/ctt/bb_videos/bb_student_videos_index.html

Maricopa Community Colleges, "Blackboard Support Materials"
http://www.mcli.dist.maricopa.edu/mlx/collection.php?id=107

Community College of Rhode Island, "WebCT Help for Students"
http://it.ccri.edu/Documentation/webct/helpstudents.shtml

University of Medicine and Dentistry of New Jersey, "Overview of WebCT"
http://www.umdnj.edu/webctweb/basics/

Bunker Hill Community College, "Overview of eCollege"
http://www.bhcc.mass.edu/eCollege/Demos/DemoWebCourse.php

OTHER RELEVANT TUTORIALS

Chapter 4.3: Navigating Online Course Materials

Chapter 4.4: Overviewing Course Materials

Chapter 4.15: Using Courseware Help or Student Help Manual

Chapter 6.5: Getting Help with Course Problems

4.15 Using Courseware Help or Student Help Manual

Introduction

Learning how your online course operates and how all the different areas work takes an investment of time and energy beyond learning and studying your course content. The courseware provides a guide and environment to access information, resources, and tools to help you succeed in the online environment. Attending a face-to-face (F2F) orientation on the courseware in a computer lab would be very important. If your institution offers an online orientation to its courseware, take the time to complete it. If not, it will be important to locate and access your courseware help or student help manual. If you can, print it and make it a deskside manual.

Online Use of the Competency/Skill

You will know how to access and use the courseware help or student help manual for guidance and assistance.

Step-by-Step Directions

Step 1. Access your online course.

Step 2. Locate the courseware help button or student help manual. Many of these help manuals have a good table of contents, index, or even a search bar to help you look for the specific help you need.

Step 3. Print out the help manual or selected pages and create a deskside reference so you can readily refer to it as needed.

Step 4. Contact the Student Help Desk, Tech Desk, Online Campus Help, or whatever online student support and services your institution may provide for any other help or assistance.

INTERNET RESOURCES

Angelo State University, "Blackboard User Manual"
http://blackboard.angelo.edu/tutorial/bbls_rel61_user.pdf

Florida State University, "Blackboard User's Guide"
http://online.fsu.edu/bb6tools/

WebCT Student Help Index
http://workbench.webct.com/web-ct/help/en/student/student_index.html

WebCT Student Resources
http://www.webct.com/oriented

Bunker Hill Community College, "eCollege Help Demo"
http://www.bhcc.mass.edu/eCollege/Demos/DemoWebCourse.php

OTHER RELEVANT TUTORIALS

Chapter 4.3: Navigating Online Course Materials

Chapter 4.4: Overviewing Course Materials

Chapter 4.14: Using Courseware Special Tools and Resources

Chapter 6.5: Getting Help with Course Problems

Chapter 6.15: Following Directions

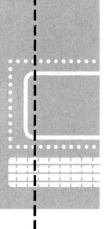

CHAPTER 5

Online Student/Learner Tasks for Online Learning

Introduction

This chapter looks at 12 online learning tasks that you will be doing as you begin, work through, and complete your online courses. Performing well on all of these tasks will ensure that you achieve success and satisfaction in all your online courses.

Four of the tasks relate to an online activity such as overviewing screen documents, study-reading Internet materials, viewing web pages, and taking notes as you read screen documents. You will also learn how to spend less time on the Internet by creating a course binder or folder, where you will keep relevant course material for offline reading, note taking, and study. This material may include your course syllabus, master schedule, directions for assignments, Internet articles, graded assignments, and any other course material that you consider useful to read and study away from an Internet connected computer.

Six of the tasks relate to writing. These include writing responses to questions that your instructor may assign weekly to test your understanding of course-required reading, writing an annotated bibliography, writing a research paper, using correct formats for citing references, proofing your writing for clarity, grammar, and spelling, and recognizing and avoiding plagiarism.

One of the tasks focuses on group work that may be required in your online course. In this task, you will learn how to function in an online group through email, chats, and discussion boards. Another task is designed to assist you with your online course assignments. A final task helps you with test taking, which may or may not take place within your online course.

5.1 Creating a Course Binder for Offline Studying

Introduction

A course binder is a three-hole-punch notebook binder or folder in which you store course material for offline reading, studying, and completing assignments. A typical course binder contains course material such as a syllabus, master schedule, directions for assignments, grading policy, assigned readings, and relevant course notes. Keep a separate course binder for each online course.

Online Use of the Competency/Skill

You will be able to read course materials and follow assignment directions offline, whenever you find time to work on your course.

Step-by-Step Directions

Step 1. Before the first week of your course or as soon after your course starts, get a three-ring notebook binder and a package of three-hole-punched computer paper. If you have access to a three-hole punch, you can use standard computer paper.

Step 2. Label the binder with the course name. If you have more than one course, consider using a binder for each course.

Step 3. Somewhere on or in the binder, write your name and telephone number in case it gets lost, so it can be returned to you.

Step 4. Make dividers for your binder to organize information according to topics such as Course Information (Master Schedule, Grading Policy, Syllabus, Weekly Lectures, Assignments, and To Do List).

Step 5. Overview all course material presented online to determine its offline use.

Step 6. Print those pages that seem useful and store in your binder.

Step 7. Add to the binder as your instructor posts lectures and assignment directions. Also add copies of your assignments as you are completing them and when they are completed and submitted to your instructor.

Step 8. Use your course binder to read and work on assignments when you don't need to access your online course.

INTERNET RESOURCES

Online Learning Success Tutorial
http://uccp.metacourse.com/next/nxstep.html

OTHER RELEVANT TUTORIALS

Chapter 4.2: Saving Course Access Information
Chapter 4.4: Overviewing Course Materials
Chapter 4.5: Printing Important Course Materials
Chapter 5.3: Taking Notes on Internet Material
Chapter 6.6: Organizing Your Course Tasks
Chapter 6.7: Creating an Efficient Learning Environment

5.2   Overviewing Screen Documents

Introduction

As an online student, you will be viewing hundreds of web pages composed mainly of text. Some documents will be many pages in length. Although you will be printing many articles relevant to your course assignments and placing them in your course binder or folder for offline reading and study, a method for overviewing screen information will help you to be more efficient and effective at recognizing useful course-related information.

Online Use of the Competency/Skill

You will know how to view, annotate, and use more efficiently Internet material that is relevant to your online course.

Step-by-Step Directions

Step 1. When you access a website, allow a minute or two to look over the screen material. Unlike the method for print material, start scanning at the top left of your screen. Most web pages follow the recommendation of web design experts to place information so that the viewer moves from left to right at the top of the page and then down to the lower left at the bottom of the page, forming an invisible "Z."

Step 2. Decide whether you will need parts of the screen for later use. Identify this material with its Internet address, so you can add that information as documentation for your quotation or paraphrase of the material.

Step 3. Decide whether you want to print this screen for offline study.

Step 4. Move your mouse over keyword lists to read any descriptive labels that pop-up when the cursor is over a word.

Step 5. Use the scroll function on your mouse to read long documents. This lets you scroll windows automatically at the speed of your choice.

Step 6. As you read, make notes, or consider printing all or portions of the screen document to make notes offline.

Step 7. Store your notes and printed screen documents in your course binder or folder for offline study.

INTERNET RESOURCES

Chris Rippel, Central Kansas Library System, "Mousing Around the Screen"
http://www.ckls.org/~crippel/computerlab/tutorials/mouse/page1.html

Idarose Luntz, Lower School Computer Lab Teacher University School, "Read Any Web Page"
http://shaker.us.edu/useweb.htm

5.3   Taking Notes on Internet Material

Introduction

During your online course, you will be viewing hundreds of Internet pages as part of your weekly reading assignment or as material to be used in a course assignment. Note taking of online material does not differ much from taking notes as you read textbook and other materials that are assigned by your instructor.

Online Use of the Competency/Skill

You will know how to effectively view material on screen and take notes that may be useful in studying or completing course assignments.

Step-by-Step Directions

Step 1. Find a note-making method (e.g., outline method, the Cornell method, concept/mind maps, or semantic maps) that appeals to you and use it. Use the note-taking function of your online courseware if it has one. Consider using a study group to share notes.

Step 2. When you access a website, before you make any notes, ask yourself what information you need for your course assignments.

Step 3. Overview the material on the screen. Scan the page for key words and phrases, highlighted areas, headings and subheads, and summaries.

Step 4. Place quotes around any material that you intend to use in an assignment.

Step 5. Paraphrase material by reading it and then rewording from memory.

Step 6. Always credit your quotes and paraphrased material using the citation format required by your instructor. This may be APA, MLA, or another format.

Step 7. When you have outlined, summarized, quoted, and paraphrased what you consider useful material, edit and proofread your work.

Step 8. Add a citation in an instructor-approved bibliographic format whenever you jot down any quote or paraphrase.

Step 9. Store notes in your course binder or folder for offline study and use.

INTERNET RESOURCES

Cal Poly SLO Study Skills Library, "Note Taking Methods"
http://www.sas.calpoly.edu/asc/ssl/notetaking.systems.html

Mind Tools, "Mind Maps—A Powerful Approach to Note Taking"
http://www.mindtools.com/pages/article/newISS_01.htm

FX Palo Alto Lab, "Shared Text Input for Note Taking on Handheld Devices"
http://www.fxpal.com/publications/FXPAL-PR-02-158.pdf

"An Internet Environment for Type-C Note Taking"
http://nr.stic.gov.tw/ejournal/ProceedingD/v12n3/122-128.pdf

Chapman University, "Hints for Good Note Taking"
http://www.chapman.edu/academics/cas/study/noteTaking.asp

Mortimer J. Adler's, "How to Mark a Book"
http://radicalacademy.com/adlermarkabook.htm

OTHER RELEVANT TUTORIALS

Chapter 2.11: Copying and Pasting
Chapter 4.4: Overviewing Course Materials
Chapter 5.1: Creating a Course Binder for Offline Studying
Chapter 5.2: Overviewing Screen Documents
Chapter 5.6: Recognizing and Avoiding Plagiarism
Chapter 6.12: Getting Help with Study Strategies

5.4   Completing Online Group Projects

Introduction

During your course, you may be asked to be part of a group to complete assignments. Knowing how to work effectively as a group member is a critical skill for successful completion of group assignments.

Online Use of the Competency/Skill

You will know how to work effectively as part of a group, either as its leader or as a participant.

Step-by-Step Directions

Step 1. Find, view, and store in your course binder or folder any directions that your instructor has provided about groups, either in the course syllabus or another course document.

Step 2. Follow directions in participating in a course group.

Step 3. Decide early on who is the group facilitator/leader and whether the group meets at scheduled times.

Step 4. Be aware of and follow group etiquette as you participate as a group member.

Step 5. If your group has a discussion board, check it often for any new information.

INTERNET RESOURCES

California Virtual Campus, "Collaborating Online"
http://www.nlight.com/Success/Collab/index.html

California State University Northridge, "Russo's Group Skills"
http://www.csun.edu/~hflrc001/groupsk.html

HCi Services, "Small Group Skills"
http://www.hci.com.au/hcisite2/toolkit/smallgro.htm

Karen Feenstra Iamnext Academics, "Study Skills: Team Work Skills for Group Projects"
http://www.iamnext.com/academics/grouproject.html

Study Guides & Strategies, "Organizing and Working on Group Projects"
http://www.studygs.net/groupprojects.htm

OTHER RELEVANT TUTORIALS

Chapter 4.7: Participating in Discussion Boards
Chapter 4.12: Accessing and Participating in a Live Chat
Chapter 4.13: Communicating Effectively in a Live Chat
Chapter 6.11: Getting Along with Your Fellow Students

5.5   Completing Online Course Assignments

Introduction

Course assignments generally make up a large part of your course grade. Course assignments may be research papers, essays, annotated bibliographies, group projects, or case studies. Being able to plan your work and work your plan is important to meet assignment deadlines.

Online Use of the Competency/Skill

You will understand how to complete an assigned course project, whether it is a research paper, annotated bibliography, case study, or group project.

message in all-uppercase letters because not only is it difficult to read, but in email it means the author is yelling. A short stretch of uppercase is acceptable where emphasis is needed. Make sure your spelling and grammar are correct. Break your message into logical paragraphs, and use sentences of sensible lengths. Avoid sending email messages with fancy backgrounds and flashy graphics. These can be distracting and annoying, especially if the recipient is on a slower connection and has to wait for your message to download.

Step 4. Use an email signature—A "Signature" is a block of text that can be added to the end of your email messages. You can set up your email application to add your signature automatically or you can choose to have it added only when you want to. You should have your signature contain your name and email address along with alternative contact information like a phone or fax number (see section 3.4). It is probably best to exclude things like graphics and emoticons.

Step 5. Be courteous. Email may be considered a less formal form of communication, but common courtesy still goes a long way. If you're asking for something, don't come across as demanding. Saying "please" will usually get better results. Similarly, if someone does something for you, a "thank you" is appreciated and will help to insure that they will be willing to help again in the future. Be careful how you say something in your email. Something said in jest may not get the expected reaction because the recipient does not have the advantage of hearing the inflection in your voice that indicates you are joking.

Step 6 Put it all together for good email etiquette. Email is a quick and easy means of communication, but how you come across will reflect on you. With concise, informative, correctly constructed, and polite communication, this reflection will be positive and will usually get better results. When you compose an email message, read it over before you send it, and ask yourself how you would react if you received it.

INTERNET RESOURCES

Learnthenet.com, "Harness Email"
http://www.learnthenet.com/english/section/email.html

Web Teacher, "Communication"
http://www.webteacher.org/windows.html

Kaitlin Sherwood's "A Beginner's Guide to Effectively Using Email"
http://www.webfoot.com/advice/email.top.html

GCF Global Learning, "Email Basics"
http://www.gcflearn.org/en/course/course_detail.asp?Course_ID=19&Course_Title=Email+Basics

3.7 Saving Email to Folders

Introduction

As an online learner, you will likely take more than one class at a time, and you will probably have many emails to and from each of your instructors. It is a good idea to organize emails of different courses so that you can easily find them if you need to refer back to them. Rather than letting all those emails accumulate in your inbox, most email applications will allow you to create multiple folders. Create a folder for each class and use it to store emails you have received and sent about the course. They will be easier for you to find if you need to in the future.

Online Use of the Competency/Skill

You will be able to create course-specific folders to help organize your email.

Step-by-Step Directions for creating folders in Microsoft Outlook

Step 1. You receive an email that you would like to file in a logical place (Figure 3.7.1).

Step 2. Highlight the root folder or choose a folder in which you would like to create a subfolder (Figure 3.7.2).

Step 3. Go to the "Menu Bar," click "File," choose "New," and then choose "Folder . . . " (Figure 3.7.3).

Step 4. Type in a name for the new folder and click "OK" (Figure 3.7.4).

Step 5. Your new folder will appear in the folder list. You can now click and drag emails into the folder (Figure 3.7.5).

Step-by-Step Directions for creating folders in Hotmail

Step 1. Click on "Manage Folders" below the "Folder List" (Figure 3.7.6).

Step 2. Go to the "Tool Bar," click on "New," and choose "Folder" (Figure 3.7.7).

Step 3. Type in a name for the new folder and click "OK" (Figure 3.7.8).

Step 4. Your newly created folder will appear in the folder list. You can now move emails into the new folder. Put a check in the "Check Box" and then go to the "Tool Bar," click on "Put in Folder," and choose "Folder Name" (Figure 3.7.9).

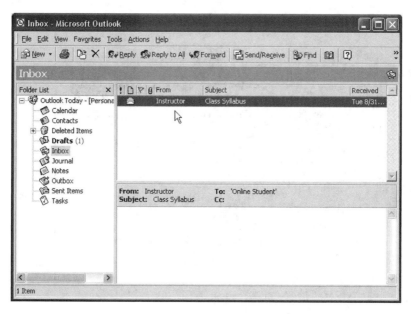

FIGURE 3.7.1 You receive an email that you want to file in a logical place.

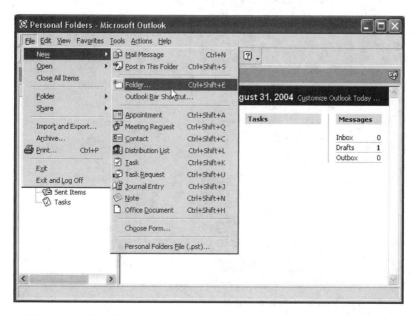

FIGURE 3.7.2 Highlight the root folder or choose a folder that you want to create a subfolder in.

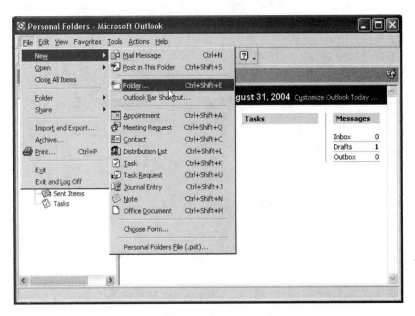

FIGURE 3.7.3 Click File > New > Folder.

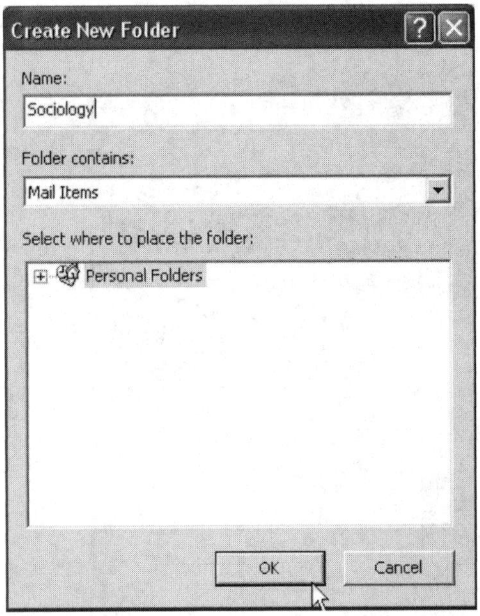

FIGURE 3.7.4 Type in a name for the new folder and click "OK."

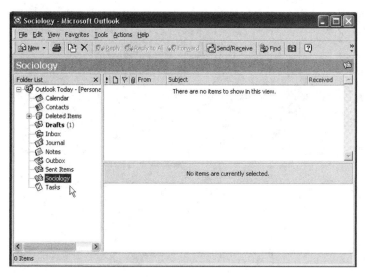

FIGURE 3.7.5 Your new folder appears. You can now click and drag emails into the folder.

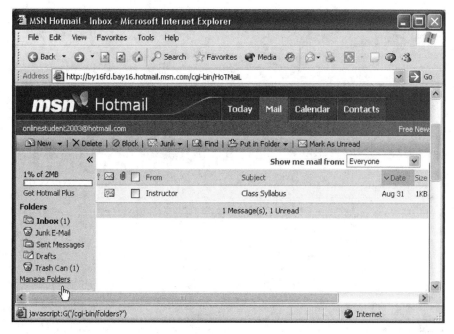

FIGURE 3.7.6 Click on "Manage Folders."

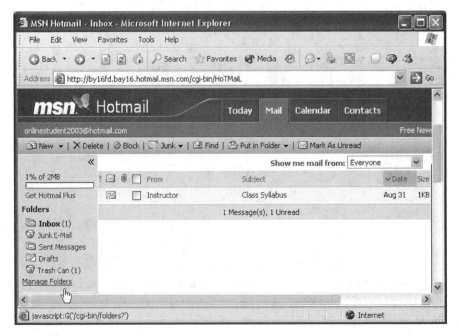

FIGURE 3.7.7 Click on New > Folder.

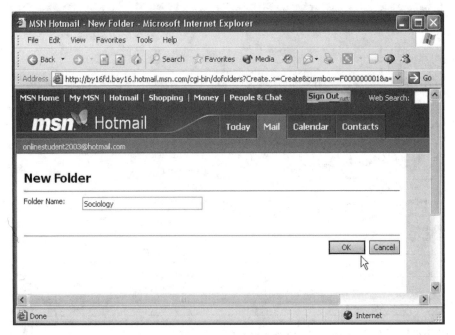

FIGURE 3.7.8 Type in a name for the new folder and click "OK."

Step-by-Step Directions

Step 1. Find and read the directions and any related material that your instructor has provided for the assignment.

Step 2. Print and store the directions in your course binder or folder so you can refer to them when you work on the assignment.

Step 3. Put any due dates assigned by your instructor on your semester calendar.

Step 4. List on your calendar any self-imposed dates for the assignment, such as completing research, completing your rough draft, and final editing and proofing of your assignment before you send to your instructor.

Step 5. Remember to save a copy of your assignment until your instructor grades the submitted version and returns it to you.

INTERNET RESOURCES

University of Texas Distance Education Center, "Guidance for Submitting Assignments"
http://www.dec.utexas.edu/onlinecourses/submitassign.html

Student Success Tips for the Online Learner
http://www.Ivytech.edu/distance/orientation/resources/success

OTHER RELEVANT TUTORIALS

Chapter 4.11: Submitting Assignments
Chapter 5.1: Creating a Course Binder for Offline Studying
Chapter 5.3: Taking Notes on Internet Material
Chapter 5.4: Completing Online Group Projects
Chapter 5.6: Recognizing and Avoiding Plagiarism
Chapter 5.8: Editing and Proofing Your Writing
Chapter 6.6: Organizing Your Course Tasks
Chapter 6.8: Managing Time for Online Learning

5.6   Recognizing and Avoiding Plagiarism

Introduction

Plagiarism is a serious offense and has serious consequences. Some students deliberately or inadvertently use material from Internet and print sources in their assignments without giving credit to the original authors. The penalty for plagiarism might be an F grade for an assignment, an F grade for the course, or at worst, dismissal from the institution. Although instructors have tools available to catch student plagiarism, they would prefer that it did not occur.

Online Use of the Competency/Skill

You will be able to recognize plagiarism, know how to avoid it, and realize the value of crediting sources in your assignments.

Step-by-Step Directions

Step 1. If you need help in recognizing plagiarism, contact your instructor or a college librarian.

Step 2. Find out if your institution has published material on student plagiarism and especially how to recognize and avoid it.

Step 3. For examples of plagiarism, access and read one or more of the Internet resources listed below.

Step 4. Ask your instructor how you should give credit to document ideas, opinions, facts, words, phrases, and sentences that are not your own.

Step 5. Before you turn in an assignment, look at all quotations or paraphrased material to see that you have acknowledged the original authors using an approved citation method.

INTERNET RESOURCES

Capital Community College, "A Statement on Plagiarism"
http://webster.commnet.edu/mla/plagiarism.shtml

University of Alberta, "Guide to Plagiarism and Cyber-Plagiarism"
http://www.library.ualberta.ca/guides/plagiarism/

Purdue University OWL, "Avoiding Plagiarism"
http://owl.english.purdue.edu/handouts/research/r_plagiar.html

University of Wisconsin Writing Center, "Quoting and Paraphrasing Sources"
http://www.wisc.edu/writing/Handbook/QuotingSources.html

Indiana University, "Plagiarism: What It Is and How to Recognize and Avoid It"
http://www.indiana.edu/~wts/pamphlets/plagiarism.shtml

OTHER RELEVANT TUTORIALS

Chapter 4.11: Submitting Assignments
Chapter 5.3: Taking Notes on Internet Material
Chapter 5.7: Using Bibliographic Formats
Chapter 5.8: Editing and Proofing Your Writing
Chapter 5.10: Writing an Annotated Bibliography
Chapter 5.11: Writing a Research Paper

5.7 Using Bibliographic Formats

Introduction

Many of your course assignments involve documenting sources that you use. Your instructor may require that you use a specific documentation format to cite your sources. Not following exactly the documentation format required for your course may cost you valuable points in your written assignments. You may be using different formats in different courses, depending on your instructor's preference for a documentation format. The most common documentation formats are those of the American Psychological Association (APA), Modern Language Association (MLA), Chicago Manual of Style, Turabian Manual for Writers of Term Papers, American Medical Association, Council of Science Editors, and American Chemical Society.

Online Use of the Competency/Skill

You will know how to document sources for your course assignments, including information you found in web pages, printed materials, emails, and course discussion board messages.

Step-by-Step Directions

Step 1. Find out from your instructor, course syllabus, or another course document which documentation format or style manual is required for the course. Note particularly what edition of a style manual is required. You may be required to use a different format for source documentation in a different online course.

Step 2. Buy or have available the latest manual or handbook for the documentation format that is required.

Step 3. Use the documentation format exactly as described in the manual or handbook or in the instructor's instructions.

Step 4. If your instructor has made up an instruction sheet with samples, store it in your course binder. If not, consider making up your own sheet as a template for your documentation.

Step 5. Remember to indicate, either as a citation or as a note, which style manual you are using to document references in your assignment.

Step 6. Before you turn in any assignment that requires documentation, edit and proofread it. If possible, get someone else to check that your documentation is correct.

INTERNET RESOURCES

Penn State University Libraries Online Reference Shelf, "Writing Resources/Style Manuals"
http://www.lias.psu.edu/gateway/referenceshelf/writ.htm#cse

Purdue University OWL, "Research and Documenting Sources"
http://owl.english.purdue.edu/handouts/research/index.html

University of Wisconsin's Writing Center, "APA Documentation"
http://www.wisc.edu/writing/Handbook/DocAPA.html

APA Online, "Electronic References"
http://www.apastyle.org/elecref.htm

Long Island University, "APA Citation Style"
http://www.liu.edu/cwis/cwp/library/workshop/citapa.htm

Long Island University, "Chicago Manual of Style Citation Guide"
http://www.liu.edu/cwis/cwp/library/workshop/citapa.htm

University of Wisconsin's Writing Center, "CBE Documentation"
http://www.wisc.edu/writing/Handbook/DocCBE.html

University of Washington, "Health Links: AMA Style Guide"
http://healthlinks.washington.edu/hsl/styleguides/ama.html

Ithaca College Library, "Turabian Samples for a Bibliography"
http://www.ithaca.edu/library/course/turabian.html

IEEE Computer Society, "Style Guide"
http://www.computer.org/author/style/

OTHER RELEVANT TUTORIALS

Chapter 5.3: Taking Notes on Internet Material
Chapter 5.6: Recognizing and Avoiding Plagiarism
Chapter 5.8: Editing and Proofing Your Writing
Chapter 5.10: Writing an Annotated Bibliography
Chapter 5.11: Writing a Research Paper
Chapter 6.4: Getting Help with Internet Research

5.8 Editing and Proofing Your Writing

Introduction

Before you submit any assignment, you must ensure that it is free of any mis-spellings and grammatical errors as well as being clear and coherent. Taking time to proofread and edit your assignments will get you the maximum point value and grade on your course assignments. Allow some time between writing an assignment and proofreading it.

Online Use of the Competency/Skill

You will know how to edit and proofread a written assignment before you submit it in your online course.

Step-by-Step Directions

Step 1. Schedule time to edit and proofread your assignment.

Step 2. Find out if your instructor has posted a writing help manual or writer's guide to acceptable writing. If so, print and store the information in your course binder or folder.

Step 3. Use a checklist, such as the one developed by the University of Wisconsin's Writing Center (see their web address in Internet Resources below), to remind you of potential problems in your writing. Print and store the information in your course binder or folder.

Step 4. Use your spell checker to catch errors, but remember that it does not flag homonyms or some typos.

Step 5. Read aloud your assignment line by line. You can find most errors easily when you read aloud. As you find an error, either correct it immediately or make a mark in the margin to alert you that there is an error to be corrected.

Step 6. Have someone else also proofread the assignment for you.

Step 7. If there is a campus writing center nearby, find out what help you can get there.

Step 8. If your institution has an online writing lab, find what help is available.

Step 9. Keep a log of your most common writing errors as a checklist for future proofing.

INTERNET RESOURCES

University of Wisconsin's Writing Center, "Twelve Common Errors: An Editing Checklist"
http://www.wisc.edu/writing/Handbook/CommonErrors.html

Purdue University's OWL, "Editing Strategies for Revision"
http://owl.english.purdue.edu/handouts/general/gl_edit.html

Purdue University's OWL, "Proofreading"
http://owl.english.purdue.edu/handouts/general/gl_proof.html

5.9   Writing Responses to Assigned Questions on Course Reading

Introduction

In almost all online courses, you are asked to read either a chapter in a textbook or an article relevant to the week's topic. In any one-semester course, you may be required to answer as few as 15 or as many as 45 questions on assigned readings. Writing responses to questions may make up a great proportion of the course grade.

Online Use of the Competency/Skill

You will know how to effectively read and answer questions on textbook or related materials.

Step-by-Step Directions

Step 1. Read and underline key words in the question. Below are some key words along with their meanings. Each key word requires a special way to respond to a question.

- *Comment*: to make personal observations intended to explain, illustrate, or criticize.
- *Compare*: to point to both similarities and differences.
- *Contrast*: to point to differences only.
- *Criticize*: not to find fault, but to judge.
- *Define*: to give meaning by setting boundaries.
- *Describe*: to list the characteristics of something.
- *Differentiate or Distinguish*: to point out particularities that enable a person to tell two or more things apart.
- *Discuss*: to present various angles, perspectives, points relating to a topic.
- *Evaluate*: to express an opinion concerning worth or merit.
- *Explain*: to make plain or understandable; to give the reasons for something.

- *Identify*: to give essential facts to show recognition and distinguish from other similar things.
- *Illustrate*: to give examples of.
- *Justify*: to provide reasons that support the validity of something.
- *Outline*: to give a brief, systematic summary.
- *Relate*: to tell or provide a narrative account.
- *Show*: to prove, to provide strong evidence supporting something.
- *State*: to indicate briefly.
- *Summarize*: to present in a condensed form.
- *Trace*: to present items chronologically.

Step 2. Overview the reading assignment using the following steps:

- Read the chapter heading or article title.
- Read subsequent section headings.
- Look at the last paragraphs for a summary or conclusion.

Step 3. Reread the question.

Step 4. Reread your assignment with pencil in hand or with a word processor open and keyboard ready. Make notes that seem to apply to the question. If you are quoting from the reading, put quotes around what you are copying.

Step 5. From your reading notes, make a brief outline of your answer.

Step 6. Always begin your answer by rewording the question to lead into your answer. For example, if the question is "Describe three major trends in current psychological theory," start your answer with an opening statement such as "Three major trends in current psychological theory are . . ."

Step 7. If possible and if you have started early on your assignment, put your answer aside for a short period of time before you complete the next step.

Step 8. Read what you have written and check for grammatical and spelling errors. Frequently, you will lose valuable points for spelling or grammatical errors.

Step 9. If your instructor requires that you document quoted material or that you reference a name or major concept from the reading material, review any instructions that you have been given to do this.

Step 10. At end of your response, list references alphabetically in whatever format your instructor has designated for the course.

Step 11. Whenever you cite an Internet reference, always check that it is accessible and use the bibliographic format that your instructor requires.

INTERNET RESOURCES

Purdue University OWL, "Writing Essay Exams"
http://owl.english.purdue.edu/handouts/general/gl_essay.html

5.10   Writing an Annotated Bibliography

Introduction

In some online courses, you may be required to research and write an annotated bibliography. An annotated bibliography is the gathering of your resources and may be a preparation for writing a research paper. Hopefully, your instructor will give you specific directions to complete this assignment.

Online Use of the Competency/Skill

You will understand how to write and submit an annotated bibliography in your online course.

Step-by-Step Directions

Step 1. As the assignment is posted, find the directions for it and then overview, print, and store them in your course binder or folder.

Step 2. Put all due dates in your course calendar. This may include the date that you must choose your topic, the date that you turn in your citations for approval, and the date that you must have your annotated bibliography emailed to your instructor or posted to the course drop box.

Step 3. Begin to collect your references. Place your work in a temporary file folder titled with the course name and number.

Step 4. Explore the Internet Resources below for information helpful to writing your annotated bibliography. Print and store useful articles in your course binder or folder.

Step 5. Depending on whether your bibliography will be descriptive or critical, begin to read and write rough drafts of your thoughts related to the articles that you have chosen.

Step 6. Submit your list of articles to your instructor if your instructor requires a list prior to writing up the annotations.

Step 7. Edit and proofread your final draft well before the submission date required by your instructor.

Step 8. Review where and how you are to submit the annotated bibliography.

Step 9. Submit your annotated bibliography on time. Save a copy.

OTHER RELEVANT TUTORIALS

Chapter 5.3: Taking Notes on Internet Material
Chapter 5.5: Completing Online Course Assignments
Chapter 5.6: Recognizing and Avoiding Plagiarism
Chapter 5.7: Using Bibliographic Formats
Chapter 5.8: Editing and Proofing Your Writing
Chapter 6.4: Getting Help with Internet Research
Chapter 6.6: Organizing Your Course Tasks

5.11 Writing a Research Paper

Introduction

In most courses, you will be required to complete some type of written assignment in which you find, read, comment, and synthesize your findings using appropriate citations for the material that you use in your paper. This assignment, whether it is called a research paper, concept paper, or term paper, will generally be considered a major assignment and will count heavily toward your final course grade.

Online Use of the Competency/Skill

You will know how to write a research paper, concept paper, or term paper.

Step-by-Step Directions

Step 1. As the assignment is posted, find the directions for it and then overview, print, and store them in your course binder or folder.

Step 2. Put all due dates in your course calendar. This may include the date that you must choose your topic, the date that you turn in your citations for approval, the date that you edit and proofread your completed paper, and the date that you must submit your research paper.

Step 3. Begin to collect your references. Place your work in a temporary folder titled with the course name and number and the phrase "Research Paper."

Step 4. Explore the Internet Resources below for information helpful to writing your research paper. Print and store useful articles in your course binder.

Step 5. Begin to read and write rough drafts of your thoughts related to the articles that you have chosen. Use a system to record quotes, paraphrases, and sources.

Step 6. Submit your research paper topic or thesis to your instructor if it must be submitted by a certain date.

Step 7. Edit and proofread your final draft well before the submission date required by your instructor.

Step 8. Review where and how you are to submit the research paper.

Step 9. Submit your research paper on time. Save a copy.

INTERNET RESOURCES

Purdue University OWL, "Research and Documenting Sources"
http://owl.english.purdue.edu/handouts/research/index.html

Capital Community College, "A Guide for Writing Research Papers Based on MLA Documentation"
http://www.ccc.commnet.edu/mla/index.shtml

OTHER RELEVANT TUTORIALS

Chapter 5.3: Taking Notes on Internet Material
Chapter 5.5: Completing Online Course Assignments
Chapter 5.6: Recognizing and Avoiding Plagiarism
Chapter 5.7: Using Bibliographic Formats
Chapter 5.8: Editing and Proofing Your Writing
Chapter 6.4: Getting Help with Internet Research
Chapter 6.6: Organizing Your Course Tasks

5.12 Preparing For and Taking Tests and Exams

Introduction

Preparing for and taking tests and major exams is not unlike what you do in a traditional class. You must manage your time, organize course material, spend time studying course material, and perhaps find or create a study group. You might take your test at a specified location under the watchful eyes of a proctor, or you might take the test online through your courseware.

Online Use of the Competency/Skill

You will know how to prepare for and take a test or exam in your online course.

Step-by-Step Directions

Step 1. As you find out when your instructor has scheduled any course tests and a final exam, write the dates in your master calendar.

Step 2. Record dates and times when you will review course material.

Step 3. Consider getting some of your fellow students to work as a group to prepare for course tests and the final exam.

Step 4. If your instructor requires you to take your tests or final exam online at a designated location with a proctor, ensure you follow your instructor's directions. Be aware you might need your photo ID to take the exam or test.

Step 5. If your instructor requires you to take your tests or exams within the courseware, note that there may be date and time limitations.

Step 6. Check the online course gradebook to ensure your completed test or exam has been entered.

INTERNET RESOURCES

Weber State University, "Advice from 'Those who Know' on Taking WSU-Online Courses"
http://wsuonline.weber.edu/studsupport/sucess_stud/advice.htm
Alamo Community College District, "Online Testing"
http://www.accd.edu/sac/history/keller/accdit/SSOtest.htm

OTHER RELEVANT TUTORIALS

Chapter 5.1: Creating a Course Binder for Offline Studying
Chapter 6.8: Managing Time for Online Learning
Chapter 6.9: Finding a Tutor
Chapter 6.12: Getting Help with Study Strategies
Chapter 6.14: Getting Help with Personal Pitfalls

CHAPTER 6

Online Learning Pitfall Solutions

Introduction

This chapter looks at fifteen pitfalls you may encounter as an online student. Although some of these problems may be similar to those you have experienced in traditional courses, they differ in the way you solve them. Other problems, such as dealing with computer stress and eye strain, are peculiar to computer and courseware use, since you will be spending considerable time at a computer. You will also need to know how to get help with any computer glitches that occur, as well as how to get help with your course assignments and Internet research problems.

    Other problems that may occur relate to knowing how to organize your course tasks and how to get help with course content. In addition, setting up a viewing and study schedule is a special time management challenge very different from any that you face in a traditional college course. Your physical environment—furniture and lighting—is another area special to online learning and studying.

    You can also learn to be more successful as an online student by finding and using study strategies and by seeking help to improve your basic reading, writing, and math competencies. This chapter also reviews some procedures for getting help with any personal problems that might affect your online work.

6.1 Coping with Computer Stress

Introduction

As an online student, you will use your computer extensively for screen viewing and for writing course-related emails, responses to reading questions, and major assignments such as an annotated bibliography and research papers. This extensive and intensive use of a computer can cause some short-term physical problems or even long-term difficulties ranging from stress to wrist damage, fatigue, shoulder pain, and muscle tenseness. The medical term for some of these physical problems is repetitive strain injury (RSI). You can lessen this stress and its related problems by making some changes in your workspace and in your viewing posture and habits.

168

Online Use of the Competency/Skill

You will know how to minimize stress and related physical problems as you work on a computer.

Step-by-Step Directions

Step 1. If this is your first prolonged use of a computer or if you are experiencing any strain or stress while using a computer, take a few moments to review the "Personal Workstation Checklist" located in Internet Resources below.

Step 2. Using the notes that you jotted down during the "Computer Stress Survey," review them and consider making changes either in your workplace or computer viewing habits.

Step 3. Adjust your monitor viewing angle so it is at a comfortable angle for minimizing stress. Adjust your chair for the best seat and back position, and adjust its height so that you are viewing the monitor at a comfortable angle.

Step 4. Use stretching exercises in "Students' Stress Busters." See Internet Resources below.

Step 5. Take a break every 20 minutes. Get out of the chair. Move around.

Step 6. Use a screen saver that automatically displays stretching exercises at predetermined intervals or upon a keyboard command.

Step 7. Use a checklist such as the Illinois State University "Personal Workstation Checklist" (see Internet Resources below) to help you evaluate and improve your work area and habits.

Step 8. Use the "Benson Relaxation Response" (see Internet Resources below) to relieve stress. It is easy to learn, requires no equipment, can be completed at or near your computer station, and most importantly, has been validated by research.

Step 9. If you tend to forget how long you are at your computer due to intense concentration on your work, set a timer to remind you to get out of your chair for a short break away from the monitor.

INTERNET RESOURCES

"Benson Relaxation Response"
http://www.oates.org/chris/stress/tip06.htm

Illinois State University, "Personal Workstation Checklist"
http://www.shs.ilstu.edu/hpo/Wellness/WellnessHome/Occupational/Ergonomics/ErgoLinks/checklist.htm

Roehampton University, "Students' Stress Busters"
http://www.roehampton.ac.uk/stressbusters/computer.asp

Paul Marxhausen, "Computer Related Repetitive Strain Injury"
http://eeshop.unl.edu/rsi.html

6.2 Minimizing Eye Strain

Introduction

During a typical three-credit online course, you spend considerable time look-ing at your computer monitor. Remember that screen viewing is more vision intensive than reading textbooks and may cause tension, eye fatigue, or stress resulting in tired, sore, burning, itching, watery, or dry eyes. In extreme cases, you may experience blurred or double vision as well as an increased sensitivity to bright lights. This vision condition has been called Computer Vision Syn-drome (CVS). This tutorial focuses on lessening or eliminating eye strain and fatigue that you may experience due to prolonged and intensive computer use.

Online Use of the Competency/Skill

You will know how to minimize eye strain from intensive computer use.

Step-by-Step Directions

Step 1. Provide a work environment at your home computer that makes for good screen viewing. This includes light and angle of viewing. Your monitor should be placed so that windows to the outside are not behind the screen or behind you. Less strain on your eye muscles will occur if you place your monitor slightly below your eye level. If you use a document holder, position it at the same height as your screen. Indirect or reflected light is best for screen viewing. Overhead fluorescent light is the least desirable type of lighting, since its flickering may affect your peripheral vision.

Step 2. Have an eye examination to determine if you might have any problems in reading text on your monitor. During this visit, tell your doctor how much time you are spending at your computer and ask about special prescription glasses for computer use. You may also want to ask about vitamins and herbal supple-ments for your eyes.

Step 3. If you find that you need eyeglasses, get a pair that is specially designed to read text at a distance of 18 to 28 inches.

Step 4. Adjust the brightness and contrast on your monitor. Controls to do this are usually located at the bottom of your monitor. Consult your monitor man-ual for directions. If you still have a glare on your screen, consider using an anti-glare filter.

Step 5. Every 10 to 15 minutes, look away from your screen and focus on some object at a distance. This change from near point to far point viewing will bring some visual relief. One recommendation is to look away from your monitor and into the distance every 20 minutes for 15 to 20 seconds.

Step 6. Consult your eye doctor if you experience any unusual eye pain or headache.

Step 7. If you have any difficulty reading text on your monitor, increase the font size. You can do this in Windows by selecting "View" on the Toolbar, and then clicking on "Zoom" to see at what size percentage your screen is set. Normally it will be set at 100%. Change it to 200% for increased font size so that you can read text more easily. While you are in the Zoom mode, note that you can also change page or text width and view a whole page or many pages. The Zoom mode offers a preview of any change that you select.

INTERNET RESOURCES

Dayton VA Medical Center, "You Can Do Something About Eyestrain"
http://www.dayton.med.va.gov/pthealth/eyestrain.html

Boston Medical Center, "Eye on Computers: Keeping Your Focus"
http://www.bu.edu/bridge/archive/1998/12-04/health.html

Larry K. Wan, O.D., "9 Steps to Reducing Computer Eyestrain"
http://www.allaboutvision.com/cvs/irritated.htm

Vision RX, "Computer Vision Syndrome (CVS)"
http://www.visionrx.com/library/enc/enc_cvs.asp

OTHER RELEVANT TUTORIALS

Chapter 5.2: Overviewing Screen Documents

Chapter 6.1: Coping with Computer Stress

Chapter 6.7: Creating an Efficient Learning Environment

6.3 Getting Help with Computer Problems

Introduction

At some time in your online course, you may experience one or more problems with your computer or with application software such as Microsoft Word, Excel, or PowerPoint. These moments of frustration can be minimized if you know where to look for help. Some problems that you may experience may be solvable with tutorials in this handbook. This tutorial lists some other steps that you can follow to solve computer and software problems.

Online Use of the Competency/Skill

You will know what to do whenever you have a hardware (desktop or laptop) or software problem.

Step-by-Step Directions

Step 1. Go to the index of this handbook to find out if it lists a tutorial for the problem that you are having. Follow the step-by-step directions to solve your problem.

Step 2. Look for help from a knowledgeable family member, neighbor, or fellow student.

Step 3. Read the manual that came with your computer or software, starting at its index to locate relevant information.

Step 4. Contact either in person, by telephone, or with email the campus help desk if one is available to you as an online student.

Step 5. Use a search engine such as Google or Yahoo to find Internet resources that may solve the problem.

Step 6. Use the specific help files that have been preloaded in some brands of computers.

Step 7. Look for software tutorial manuals at a computer store or a local bookstore. Many publications are designed specifically for beginning computer users. They contain visuals (screen shots) or have an accompanying CD, often with visuals and spoken directions.

Step 8. Find and use the operating system or application specific Help function. You can usually do this quickly by pressing the "F1" key on your keyboard.

INTERNET RESOURCES

Florida Gulf Coast University, "Technology Skills Orientation"
http://www.fgcu.edu/support/office2000/word/

EducationOnlineforComputers.com, "Education Online for Computer Software"
http://www.educationonlineforcomputers.com/

OTHER RELEVANT TUTORIALS

All Chapter 2 tutorials

6.4 Getting Help with Internet Research

Introduction

Although you will still use the library and its printed resources for many of the assignments in your online course, most of your research will be on the Internet using Google, Yahoo, and other search engines. Knowing how to use the Internet for your research will assist you in completing your assignments. Your research will be more productive if you use librarians—campus or local, face-to-face, or online—to assist you with your research.

Online Use of the Competency/Skill

You will know how to use the Internet to find material relevant to a course assignment.

Step-by-Step Directions

Step 1. Look for research suggestions that may be listed in your course materials—assignment directions, course texts, bibliography, and syllabus.

Step 2. Before starting your online research, develop an alphabetical list of words and phrases that might yield useful results for your course assignment. This alpha list will be useful in locating information relevant to your assignment topic.

Step 3. As you use search engines, keep a record of the search terms that you have used and the results or lack of results from your search terms.

Step 4. Make an appointment with a librarian on a college campus or at your local library. Share your alphabetical list of research terms with the librarian. Take notes on recommendations made by the librarian.

Step 5. Use the course-required bibliographic format to record sources that you find useful for your assignment. This will ensure that you do not plagiarize material you use in your assignment.

INTERNET RESOURCES

UC Berkeley Library, "Finding Information on the Internet: A Tutorial"
http://www.lib.berkeley.edu/TeachingLib/Guides/Internet/FindInfo.html

Purdue University OWL, "Searching the World Wide Web"
http://owl.english.purdue.edu/internet/search/

University at Albany Universities Library, "Internet Tutorials"
http://library.albany.edu/internet/

Monash University, "Library Online Tutorials"
http://www.lib.monash.edu.au/vl/www/wwwcon.htm

6.5   Getting Help with Course Problems

Introduction

Inevitably you will encounter problems with the course software that you are using—Blackboard, WebCT, e-College, and other courseware. The problem may be in attempting to develop your home page with a digital photo and text material. The problem may be posting to a discussion board, using the course chat function, submitting assignments, or navigating through the course buttons. This tutorial will give you some alternative ways to solve these problems.

Online Use of the Competency/Skill

You will know how to get help whenever you have a problem with your online courseware and its functions.

Step-by-Step Directions

Step 1. Immediately communicate with your course instructor or a course teaching assistant to ask for help with your specific problem.

Step 2. Email another student in your course to ask for help.

Step 3. Look in your course documents for any help directions that the instructor has written and published for your course.

Step 4. Find the courseware student manual. Look in its index for help with your problem. Follow its directions to solve your courseware problem.

Step 5. Access the website of your online institution and see if it contains tutorials that are specific to the courseware problem you are encountering.

Step 6. Contact your institution's help desk if available.

INTERNET RESOURCES

The University of Texas at Austin, "Blackboard Tutorials Student Manual"
http://www.utexas.edu/academic/blackboard/tutorials/student/

East Carolina University, "Blackboard Tutorials"
http://www.ecu.edu/elearning/orientation/Blackboard/Bbtutorial.htm

Regent University, "Blackboard Tutorials" (Video)
http://www.regent.edu/general/student_orientation/tutorials/blackboard.cfm

University of Houston Victoria, "Vista Tutorials"
http://www.uhv.edu/webct/students/orientation/tutorials/vista_tutorial.htm

California State University, Chico, "WebCT Tutorial"
http://www.csuchico.edu/stcp/online/tutorial/

WebCT, "Student Tour"
http://www.webct.com/oriented/ViewContent?contentID=1805985&pageName=student_tour3/intro.html

OTHER RELEVANT TUTORIALS

Chapter 4.4: Overviewing Course Materials

Chapter 4.6: Using the Course Syllabus

Chapter 4.15: Using Courseware Help or Student Help Manual

Chapter 6.3: Getting Help with Computer Problems

Chapter 6.15: Following Directions

6.6   Organizing Your Course Tasks

Introduction

Knowing how to organize academic tasks and, in particular, online course tasks involves managing your time and following directions for course assignments. If you always remember to plan your work and then work your plan, you will be able to complete course assignments efficiently and effectively.

Online Use of the Competency/Skill

You will know how to organize course tasks such as a paper, group project, or preparation for a test or exam.

Step-by-Step Directions

Step 1. Find the directions for the task.

Step 2. Print and store all directions in your course binder or folder under the title of the assignment.

Step 3. Reread the directions and underline key information such as the due dates of assignments and any special requirements imposed by your instructor.

Step 4. Start a computer file or a paper folder for each assignment as a place to keep all information, your thoughts, any research notes, and rough drafts relevant to the assignment.

Step 5. As you work on your assignment, place all relevant material in your file or folder.

Step 6. Allow time on your schedule to review your assignment for clarity, spelling, and grammar.

Step 7. Allow time on your schedule for someone else to review your assignment for clarity, spelling, and grammar.

INTERNET RESOURCES

San Diego State University, "Online Learning: How to Get the Most Out of Your Online Learning Experience"
http://defcon.sdsu.edu/1/objects/online/

Muskingum College CAL, "Organization"
http://www.muskingum.edu/~cal/database/general/organization.html

Psychological Skills Press, "Organization"
http://www.psyskills.com/add01.htm

OTHER RELEVANT TUTORIALS

Chapter 4.11: Submitting Assignments
Chapter 5.1: Creating a Course Binder for Offline Studying
Chapter 5.4: Completing Online Group Projects
Chapter 5.5: Completing Online Course Assignments
Chapter 6.8: Managing Time for Online Learning
Chapter 6.12: Getting Help with Study Strategies

6.7   Creating an Efficient Learning Environment

Introduction

Your choice of a study environment—location, furnishings, learning and study tools, noise, air, and body comfort—can make a difference in how much and how well you study. All these factors greatly affect your learning and study efficiency and effectiveness.

Online Use of the Competency/Skill

You will know how to develop an environment that is conducive to quiet study and course activity.

Step-by-Step Directions

Step 1. Complete a study environment analysis such as the one at Virginia Tech listed in Internet Resources below.

Step 2. Based on the analysis, choose your best place to study.

Step 3. Make any changes in your study environment based on the suggestions in "How to Modify Your Study Environment I" (see Internet Resources below).

INTERNET RESOURCES

Virginia Tech, "Study Environment Analysis"
http://www.ucc.vt.edu/stdysk/studydis.html

Virginia Tech, "Control of the Environment"
http://www.ucc.vt.edu/stdysk/control.html

University of Texas at Austin Learning Center, "How to Modify Your Study Environment I"
http://www.utexas.edu/student/utlc/makinggrade/modifystudyenvironment.html

OTHER RELEVANT TUTORIALS

Chapter 4.1: Accessing Your Course Anytime, Anywhere

Chapter 5.1: Creating a Course Binder for Offline Studying

Chapter 6.1: Coping with Computer Stress

Chapter 6.2: Minimizing Eye Strain

Chapter 6.8: Managing Time for Online Learning

6.8   Managing Time for Online Learning

Introduction

As you make up your course learning and study schedule, note that you are scheduling three different types of time: (1) screen viewing time, (2) study time, and (3) course projects time. Since late assignments can result in loss of grade points, how you manage your time is crucial to course success. In addition, if you have a problem with procrastination—described as "the thief of time"—you need to recognize it and have some ways to deal with it.

Online Use of the Competency/Skill

You will know how to manage your time effectively and how to overcome procrastination.

Step-by-Step Directions

Step 1. Read the syllabus and course schedule and add to your calendar the date and title of each assignment.

Step 2. Have your calendar of assignments near your computer to remind you of these tasks.

Step 3. If you use a Day-Timer or other desk or pocket calendar, write each task in its due date page. If your courseware has a calendar and task reminder function, use it so that whenever you access your course, you see your calendar and due dates of any assignments.

Step 4. Since you may be in a different time zone than your instructor and fellow students, keep a clock next to your computer that is set to the host time of your course so that you do not miss any deadlines for assignments or scheduled times for chats.

Step 5. Find your "procrastination quotient" by completing the University of Texas at Austin's self-report survey. See Internet Resources below. If your quotient is 21 and above, get help from a college counselor.

Step 6. As a daily routine task, overview your time management schedule and your list of "to do" tasks. This is best accomplished as an early morning preview to determine what you must do, and as a late afternoon or evening review to check what you have done and what was not done and must be carried over to the next day.

Step 7. As a weekly routine, review your performance every Saturday. Make note of any "catch-up" course work to be scheduled for completion. Each Sunday, preview your course schedule and any instructor announcements to find out what study time, assignment time, or exam preparation time you must schedule during the coming week.

INTERNET RESOURCES

University of Texas at Austin, "Procrastination Quotient"
http://www.utexas.edu/student/utlc/makinggrade/pquotient.html

University of Nebraska, "Thirteen Timely Tips for More Effective Personal Time Management"
http://www.ianr.unl.edu/pubs/homemgt/nf172.htm

University of Guelph, "Learning Time"
http://www.webshops.uoguelph.ca/learningtime/

Marin Community College, "Managing Time & Setting Priorities"
http://www.marin.cc.ca.us/~don/Study/5time.html

Oregon State University Academic Success Tutorial, "Procrastination"
http://success.oregonstate.edu/study/procrastination.cfm?A=0

OTHER RELEVANT TUTORIALS

Chapter 5.1: Creating a Course Binder for Offline Studying

Chapter 6.6: Organizing Your Course Tasks

Chapter 6.7: Creating an Efficient Learning Environment

6.9 Finding a Tutor

Introduction

At some time during your course, you may feel that you do not understand what is being taught. You may find that you need help with the course subject matter. You may be having difficulty solving science or math problems. You may realize that your writing or reading skills are not up to the expectations of your course instructor. You may consider getting some help in one or more of these areas—help that is available if you only reach out for it.

Online Use of the Competency/Skill

You will know how to get tutoring help whenever you have any difficulty with course subject matter, written assignments, or math problems.

Step-by-Step Directions

Step 1. Look at your course syllabus to see if your instructor has provided any suggestions for tutorial help. This may be a teaching assistant or a content tutor. If so, contact the appropriate tutor immediately.

Step 2. Access the institutional website to see if tutorial assistance is available for your course either through the website or at the institution's tutor center.

Step 3. Email your course instructor for assistance in finding a tutor.

Step 4. Through your course email, ask your fellow students for some possible leads to a tutor.

Step 5. Explore the Internet Resources below for online tutoring.

INTERNET RESOURCES

TutorNation
http://www.tutornation.com/index1.asp

TutorsDirectory
http://www.tutors-online.co.uk/

Tutors Online
http://www.dctech.com/tutors/index.php

Tutor.com
http://www.tutor.com/

OTHER RELEVANT TUTORIALS

Chapter 4.6: Using the Course Syllabus
Chapter 5.12: Preparing For and Taking Tests and Exams
Chapter 6.12: Getting Help with Study Strategies

6.10   Getting Along with Your Instructor

Introduction

As an online student, most of your communication with your instructor will be through email, chat, and discussion boards, where you should always be courteous and professional. Although you are invisible when you access your online courses, your language is not. How you address and respond to your instructor is an important consideration. Rules of courtesy and netiquette ought to be your guide as you interact with your online instructor.

Online Use of the Competency/Skill

You will know how to maintain a good working relationship with your instructor.

Step-by-Step Directions

Step 1. Follow all directions in your course syllabus, announcements, course documents, and discussion boards to minimize any problems with your instructor.

Step 2. If you have a problem with your instructor or teaching assistant, think before you compose an email, start a chat session, or make a telephone call to the person to discuss the problem. Be diplomatic. Be polite. Avoid any snarl words.

Step 3. Know the procedures that your instructor has published either in the course syllabus, announcements, or discussion boards to resolve any questions or conflicts.

Step 4. Use your word processor to write emails and discussion board comments, and reread them before sending them to ensure that you are being courteous. If it is an email communication, place it in your Draft folder so you can go back to it later to reflect on your writing prior to sending.

INTERNET RESOURCES

"Netiquette Home Page"
http://www.albion.com/netiquette/

Arlene Rinaldi, **"User Guide and Netiquette Index"**
http://www.fau.edu/netiquette/net/

Idaho Digital Learning Academy, **"Orientation to Online Learning:
Netiquette"**
http://idla.k12.id.us/Policies/IDLA_Student_Center_Netiquette.htm

OTHER RELEVANT TUTORIALS

Chapter 4.6: Using the Course Syllabus

Chapter 4.8: Netiquette in Discussion Boards

Chapter 4.13: Communicating Effectively in a Live Chat

Chapter 6.14: Getting Help with Personal Pitfalls

6.11 Getting Along with Your Fellow Students

Introduction

Your language in an email or discussion board reflects back on you. It is important that you treat your fellow students with respect as you would want to be treated. It is just as inappropriate in an online course to make jokes or offensive remarks about race, nationality, religion, sexual preference, physical condition, or communication skills as it is in a traditional classroom. Moreover, your remarks are visible, perhaps all semester, for your instructor and your fellow students to view.

Online Use of the Competency/Skill

You will know how to maintain a good working relationship with your fellow students.

Step-by-Step Directions

Step 1. Follow all directions in your course syllabus, announcements, course documents, and discussion boards that relate to course communications to minimize any problems with your fellow students.

Step 2. If you have a problem with another student and want to discuss it with the person, think before you compose an email, start a chat session, or make a telephone call. Be diplomatic and polite.

Step 3. Know the procedures that your instructor has published either in the course syllabus, announcements, or discussion boards to resolve any questions or conflicts.

Step 4. Use your word processor to write emails and discussion board comments, and reread them before sending them to ensure that you are being courteous. If it is an email communication, place it in your Draft folder so you can go back to it later to reflect on your writing before you send it.

INTERNET RESOURCES

"Netiquette Home Page"
http://www.albion.com/netiquette/

Arlene Rinaldi, "User Guide and Netiquette Index"
http://www.fau.edu/netiquette/net/

Idaho Digital Learning Academy, "Orientation to Online Learning: Netiquette"
http://idla.k12.id.us/Policies/IDLA_Student_Center_Netiquette.htm

OTHER RELEVANT TUTORIALS

Chapter 4.8: Netiquette in Discussion Boards
Chapter 4.13: Communicating Effectively in a Live Chat
Chapter 5.4: Completing Online Group Projects
Chapter 6.14: Getting Help with Personal Pitfalls

6.12   Getting Help with Study Strategies

Introduction

To be successful in online courses, you must have some knowledge of study strategies that you can use to organize course tasks. You want to make the best use of your time as you study course material, prepare for and take tests and exams, make course notes for study, memorize facts and concepts, complete assignments, and research, write, edit, and proofread course papers.

Online Use of the Competency/Skill

You will know how to improve your study strategies for increased course success.

Step-by-Step Directions

Step 1. Overview the course syllabus to see if your instructor has suggested or published any study assistance material that is available for you should you need help.

Step 2. Look for any study help documents that your instructor has provided for the course.

Step 3. Look for any external links to study strategy materials—Internet or print—that your instructor has added to the course.

Step 4. Look on your institutional website for study strategy tutorials or links to Internet study strategy resources.

Step 5. Look on your course site for any external links to study strategy materials.

Step 6. Use a search engine like Google, Yahoo, or Vivisimo to locate study strategy tutorials or handouts. In the Search box, type the specific study strategy term, such as "critical thinking," to find web pages. Bookmark these websites so they are handy when you need to refer to them.

Step 7. Use one or more of the Internet resources listed below for useful study strategy tutorials and handouts. Print and store them in your course binder or folder for easy referral.

INTERNET RESOURCES

"Study Guides and Strategies"
http://www.studygs.net

Utah State Academic Resource Center, "Online Learning Center"
http://www.usu.edu/arc/index.php?site_id=7

Wilton High School, "Chemistry Coach"
http://www.chemistrycoach.com/lbe4.htm

Chemeketa Community College, "Howtostudyorg"
http://www.howtostudy.org/

6.13 Improving Your Basic Skills

Introduction

If your instructor suggests that you need help with basic skills in reading, writing, critical thinking, or math, help is available but you must reach out to find and use it. Do this before you decide to drop out of the course. However, realize that you will be spending extra time to develop your basic skills and need to find a place for this special development time in your schedule.

Online Use of the Competency/Skill

You will know how to find help with basic skills in reading, writing, critical thinking, or math.

Step-by-Step Directions

Step 1. As soon as you know that your basic skills are not up to course standards, look for help. You may be told by your instructor that you require help with your reading, writing, or math skills or you may realize that you need help from the grades and critiques on your course assignments.

Step 2. Ask your instructor where you might get assistance, either print or Internet, with the particular skill that needs improvement.

Step 3. If you are on or near a campus, find its learning or tutorial center and get help there. Such centers may have self-help computer or media materials that you can use.

Step 4. If you think that you can develop these skills on your own, search the Internet using specific search terms to find tutorials. There are basic materials on the web that can help you master the fundamentals of math, reading, spelling, writing, and for many required college subjects such as physics, chemistry, and others.

Step 5. For more self-help print materials, use your campus or local library as well as campus and local bookstores.

INTERNET RESOURCES

Oracle Think Quest, "Learn Physics Today"
http://library.thinkquest.org/10796/ch1/ch1.htm

Dan's Math Lessons, "Math Basic Skills"
http://home.earthlink.net/~djbach/basic.html

Learning Support Centers in Higher Education, "Links to Traditional Learning & Study Strategies Web Pages"
http://www.pvc.maricopa.edu/~lsche/resources/online/ol_traditional.htm

OTHER RELEVANT TUTORIALS

Chapter 6.8: Managing Time for Online Learning
Chapter 6.9: Finding a Tutor
Chapter 6.12: Getting Help with Study Strategies
Chapter 6.14: Getting Help with Personal Pitfalls

6.14 Getting Help with Personal Pitfalls

Introduction

During your online course, you may feel stressed, unmotivated, extremely tired, and unable to cope with course assignments and personal or family problems. The worst thing you can do is ignore the problem and think it will go away. Help is out there, but you need to look for it and make the effort to connect with available resources.

Online Use of the Competency/Skill

You will know how to find help if you feel overly stressed, have a sense of helplessness, feel constantly tired, or think that what you are doing is a waste of time and has no purpose or value.

Step-by-Step Directions

Step 1. If your problem is a minor one of motivation or stress, ask a campus counselor to recommend self-help material and activities to lessen the problem. Or try one of the Internet Resources below.

Step 2. Communicate with a family member, friend, fellow student, or minister, and discuss your problem.

Step 3. Get help either through your course instructor or through the counseling center at your campus.

Step 4. If your problem is physical, make an appointment to visit the campus health center or to see your doctor for assistance.

INTERNET RESOURCES

Stress Oasis, "Benson Relaxation Response"
http://www.oates.org/chris/stress/tip06.htm

Roehampton University, "Students' Stress Busters"
http://www.roehampton.ac.uk/stressbusters/computer.asp

OTHER RELEVANT TUTORIALS

Chapter 6.1: Coping with Computer Stress
Chapter 6.10: Getting Along with Your Instructor
Chapter 6.11: Getting Along with Your Fellow Students

6.15 Following Directions

Introduction

During your online course, you will be viewing directions from your course instructor to complete an assignment. It is imperative to find, read, understand, and follow the specific guidance for each assignment. The grade you receive on your assignments depends on how well you read and follow directions.

Online Use of the Competency/Skill

You will know how to follow directions to effectively complete a course assignment.

Step-by-Step Directions

Step 1. If you are interested in finding out how well you follow directions, take the Directions Quiz by Anna Purnell. See Internet Resources below.

Step 2. Read, print, and store in your course binder or folder all directions from your course instructor.

Step 3. Read all directions carefully and make notes on your print copy that indicate whether you need to ask your instructor about the directions if you do not understand them.

Step 4. Keep a copy of the directions in front of you as you do an assignment. Refer to them constantly to see that you are following the instructor's directions.

Step 5. Review your assignment prior to submission to ensure that you have followed the specific directions of your instructor.

Step 6. Overview the Internet Resources for this tutorial. Print and store whatever seems useful for you to refer to as an aid in following directions.

INTERNET RESOURCES

Anna Purnell, Madison Area Technical College, "Following Directions"
http://www.apurnell.com/images/FOLLOWING%20DIRECTIONS.htm

"How Well Can You Follow Directions"
http://www.justriddlesandmore.com/direct.html

OTHER RELEVANT TUTORIALS

Chapter 4.5: Printing Important Course Materials

Chapter 4.11: Submitting Assignments

Chapter 5.1: Creating a Course Binder for Offline Studying

Chapter 6.5: Getting Help with Course Problems

Conclusion

Congratulations! Upon mastering all the tutorials within the *Online Student Skills and Strategies Handbook* you are set not only to survive and succeed in the online education environment, but will excel in all of your online courses. The specific tutorials in the handbook will give you the necessary skills and strategies to make your online education a successful and enjoyable learning experience.

Keep the *Online Student Skills and Strategies Handbook* by your computer so when you encounter a course activity or assignment problem, you can turn to the Table of Contents or index in this handbook where you will find the page references to an applicable tutorial that takes you step-by-step through directions that you can follow.

Being an online student requires great discipline and self-motivation, and some unique and specific skills and competencies that are quite different from the traditional learning skills that are necessary for success in traditional face-to-face (F2F) courses. This handbook provides you with specific and practical step-by-step tutorials, which will greatly enhance your online learning experience.

The *Online Student Skills and Strategies Handbook* gives you the practical skills to meet the challenges of online education and prepares you for a successful and rewarding online learning experience. As you progress through your learning, the skills you have learned in this handbook, those that once seemed foreign and difficult, will become second nature. You will build on these skills and they will carry you through your online education and beyond. Now go forth and pursue your online education . . . relentlessly!

APPENDIX A
Webliography

Internet resources are listed by chapter in the list that follows. Occasionally a website will be discontinued; however, you may be able to find an alternate website on the Web Companion site that the publisher has made available for this handbook.

Chapter 2: Computer Tasks for Online Learning

University of Toledo Distance & eLearning, "Minimum Computer Requirements"
http://www.dl.utoledo.edu/minimum_require.htm

Florida Atlantic University, "Minimum Computer Requirements"
http://www.itss.fau.edu/computer.htm

Southwest Missouri State University, "Minimum Computer Requirements"
http://www.smsuonline.smsu.edu/getready/mincompreqs.htm

AOL Webmaster Info, "About Cookies"
http://webmaster.info.aol.com/aboutcookies.html

FindTutorials.com, "What are Cookies"
http://tutorials.findtutorials.com/read/id/51/headline/What+are+Cookies%3F

Tech Encyclopedia, "Javascript"
http://www.tech-encyclopedia.com/JavaScript.htm

Web Teacher, "Web Basics"
http://www.webteacher.org/windows.html

Yahoo
http://www.yahoo.com

Find Tutorials, "Browsing Web Pages"
http://tutorials.findtutorials.com/read/category/10/id/405

How Stuff Works, "How Internet Search Engines Work"
http://computer.howstuffworks.com/search-engine.htm

Widener University Wolfgang Memorial Library, "Accessing Web Pages Using Netscape"
http://www2.widener.edu/Wolfgram-Memorial-Library/pyramid/wwwawpun.htm

Oracle Think Quest, "Breaking Through the Ice on the Internet"
http://library.thinkquest.org/24114/

Internet4classrooms, "Using Favorites Effectively"
http://www.internet4classrooms.com/entry_level_pc_ie_fav.htm

Shasta College, "Bookmark a Favorite Website"
http://online.shastacollege.edu/webct/survivalguide/16bookmark.htm

FindTutorials.com, "Understanding the World Wide Web (Part 1)"
http://tutorials.findtutorials.com/read/query/plug-ins/id/52

Shasta College, "Downloading and Plug-ins"
http://online.shastacollege.edu/webct/survivalguide/19download.htm

Cornell University, "Clearing Cache Settings"
http://campusgw.library.cornell.edu/newhelp/technical/errors/answers/clearcache.html

FindTutorials.com, "Customizing the Browser"
http://tutorials.findtutorials.com/read/query/clearing%20cache/id/407

About.com, "How to Change Your Windows 2000 Screen Resolution"
http://windows.about.com/c/ht/00/07/How_Change_Windows_20000962933004.htm

Learnthenet.com, "Master the Basics: Monitor Settings"
http://www.learnthenet.com/english/html/06settng.htm

Microsoft.com, "Windows XP Professional Product Documentation"
http://www.microsoft.com/resources/documentation/windows/xp/all/proddocs/en-us/display_change_screen_resolution.mspx

Computertim Technologies, "Zoom"
http://www.computertim.com/howto/article.php?topic=word&idn=100

FindTutorials.com, "Managing Folders"
http://tutorials.findtutorials.com/read/query/creating%20folders/id/466

DMIA.org, "How to copy and paste"
http://www.dmia.org/tutorial/basic_internet_tut/copy_paste_tut.html

FindTutorials.com, "Word 2002 (XP) Moving and Copying Text"
http://tutorials.findtutorials.com/read/query/copying%20&%20pasting/id/342

Planet PDF, "Getting text out of your PDF"
http://www.planetpdf.com/enterprise/article.asp?ContentID=6309

FindTutorials.com, "Windows 2000 Applications (Page 2)"
http://tutorials.findtutorials.com/read/query/saving%20files/id/333/p/2

Web Institute for Teachers, "Computer Basics, All About Windows Specific Information"
http://webinstituteforteachers.org/2000/curriculum/homeroommodules/compBasics/WinPage.htm#Windows%20on%20Windows

Mark Merickel, OSU Uploading Files in Discussion Forums
http://oregonstate.edu/instruct/pte/tutorial/forums/attach.htm

Indiana University, "In Microsoft Word and Corel WordPerfect for Windows, what file formats can I save in and convert from?"
http://kb.indiana.edu/data/ahkn.html

Ohio University, "Converting Documents"
http://www.ohiou.edu/independent/tutorial/C_c.htm

Wellesley College, "Opening and Saving documents in various formats with Microsoft Word"
http://www.wellesley.edu/Computing/Word/Conversion/wordToOther.html

Computertim Technologies, "Switch Between Applications"
http://www.computertim.com/howto/article.php?topic=windows&idn=53

Web Institute for Teachers, "Computer Basics, All About Windows Specific Information"
http://webinstituteforteachers.org/2000/curriculum/homeroommodules/compBasics/WinPage.htm#Windows%20on%20Windows

Arizona State University, "Securing Your Workstation"
http://www.west.asu.edu/it/start/wksecurity.htm

Carnegie Mellon University, CERT Coordination Center, "Home Computer Security"
http://www.cert.org/homeusers/HomeComputerSecurity/

Wellesley College, "Securing Your Computer"
http://www.wellesley.edu/Computing/Security/Spybot http://www.safer-networking.org/en/index.html

Ad-aware
http://www.lavasoftusa.com/software/adaware/

ZoneAlarm
http://www.zonelabs.com

Chapter 3: Email Tasks for Online Learning

Learnthenet.com, "Harness Email"
http://www.learnthenet.com/english/section/email.html

Web Teacher, "Communication"
http://www.webteacher.org/windows.html

Kaitlin Sherwood's, "A Beginner's Guide to Effectively Using Email"
http://www.webfoot.com/advice/email.top.html

GCF Global Learning, "Email Basics"
http://www.gcflearn.org/en/course/course_detail.asp?Course_ID=19&Course_Title=Email+Basics

Free email accounts
http://email.about.com/od/freeemailreviews/

Chapter 4: Online Course Tasks for Online Learning

Delaware Woman Online, "Anytime/Anywhere Learning"
http://www.delawarewoman.com/200204/anytimeany.html

Learning in the New Economy, "Anywhere, Anytime, Take-it-to-go Learning"
http://www.linezine.com/3.1/features/cwdfmw.htm

Learnthenet.com, "Online Learning"
http://www.learnthenet.com/english/html/83online.htm

GCF Global Learning, "Internet Lessons"
http://www.gcflearn.org/gcf_classes/internet/index.asp

University of South Dakota Trio Tutorials, "Saving Your Files"
http://www.usd.edu/trio/tut/saving/index.html

Duke University School of Nursing Tutorials, "Managing Your Files"
http://www.duke.edu/~dhewitt/tutorials/explorer/explor.html

Washington Online, "An Example of Online Course Navigation"
http://www.waol.org/learnToLearn/Module1/mod1_01.htm

St. Petersburg College, "An Example of WebCT Course Navigation"
http://instcomp.spjc.edu/webcttutorialv4/movingaround/movies/course
_navigation/

Florida Metropolitan University, "An Example of eCollege Course Navigation"
http://www.fmuonline.com/pdf/handbook.pdf

CTLE, University of Scranton—Blackboard Navigation
http://academic.scranton.edu/department/ctle/tutorials/technology/
blackboard-nav/

Boise State University, "Overview of Blackboard"
http://itc.boisestate.edu/orient/overview.htm

University of Wales—Printing Course Documents
http://alto.aber.ac.uk/bb/helpsheets/student_print.asp

UC College Prep, Online Learning Success Tutorial
http://uccp.metacourse.com/next/nxstep.html

University of Medicine & Dentistry of New Jersey, "Overview of WebCT"
http://www.umdnj.edu/webctweb/basics/

Bunker Hill Community College, "Overview of eCollege"
http://www.bhcc.mass.edu/eCollege/Demos/DemoWebCourse.php

Find Tutorials, "Printing Documents"
http://tutorials.findtutorials.com/

Study Guides and Strategies, "Succeeding in Distance Education Courses"
http://www.studygs.net/distanceed.htm

Cleveland State University, "Course Syllabus"
http://www.csuohio.edu/gradcollege/student/handbook/chapters/syllabus.htm

Mansfield University Center for Effective Teaching, "Getting On the Syllabus"
http://www.mnsfld.edu/~effteach/99decAcronym.html

Washtenaw Community College, "Participating in Discussion Boards"
https://www.wccnet.edu/resources/computerresources/blackboard/pdf/Discussion_Boards.pdf

Netiquette, "Netiquette for Discussion Groups"
http://www.albion.com/netiquette/book/0963702513p65.html

Online Netiquette, "Netiquette Matters"
http://www.onlinenetiquette.com/netiquette_guide.html

Netiquette Now, "Netiquette for Newsgroups, Bulletin Boards and Discussion"
http://www.advicemeant.com/netiquet/usenet.shtml

University of Texas, "Using the Discussion Board"
http://www.utexas.edu/academic/blackboard/tutorials/pdfs/Discussion.pdf

University of Texas Distance Education Center, "Guidance for Submitting Assignments"
http://www.dec.utexas.edu/onlinecourses/submitassign.html

Dakota County Technical College, "Example of Submitting Assignments in WebCT"
http://www.dctc.mnscu.edu/olc/assign.html

UCLA Extension, "Example of Submitting Assignments in Blackboard"
http://www.victoriawebpages.com/viewlets/assess/assess_viewlet.html

Case Western Reserve University, "Blackboard Communication Tools"
http://www.cwru.edu/net/csg/CI/virchat.html

Oregon State University, "Blackboard Virtual Classroom"
http://oregonstate.edu/instruct/coursedev/tutorials/Bb/virtual_classroom.htm

Palm Beach Community College, "WebCT Communication"
http://www.pbcc.edu/faculty/ottp/WebCT_site/7_Communiction/7communemenu.htm

Homepage Made Easy, "Communicating Online"
http://www.homepagemadeeasy.com/communicate4.html

University of Wisconsin-Madison, "Communicating in an Online Environment"
http://wiscinfo.doit.wisc.edu/ltde/ORFI/ces/print/communicating.htm

Mentor Place, "Common Issues in Online Communication"
http://www.mentorplace.org/MPT/MPTCCommonIssues.htm

Ball State University, "Blackboard Tutorials"
http://web.bsu.edu/ctt/bb_videos/bb_student_videos_index.html

Maricopa Community Colleges, "Blackboard Support Materials"
http://www.mcli.dist.maricopa.edu/mlx/collection.php?id=107

Community College of Rhode Island, "WebCT Help for Students"
http://it.ccri.edu/Documentation/webct/helpstudents.shtml

University of Medicine and Dentistry of New Jersey, "Overview of WebCT"
http://www.umdnj.edu/webctweb/basics/

Bunker Hill Community College, "Overview of eCollege"
http://www.bhcc.mass.edu/eCollege/Demos/DemoWebCourse.php

Angelo State University, "Blackboard User Manual"
http://blackboard.angelo.edu/tutorial/bbls_rel61_user.pdf

Florida State University, "Blackboard User's Guide"
http://online.fsu.edu/bb6tools/

WebCT Student Help Index
http://workbench.webct.com/web-ct/help/en/student/student_index.html

WebCT Student Resources
http://www.webct.com/oriented

Bunker Hill Community College, "eCollege Help Demo"
http://www.bhcc.mass.edu/eCollege/Demos/DemoWebCourse.php

Chapter 5: Online Student/Learner Tasks for Online Learning

Chris Rippel, Central Kansas Library System, "Mousing Around the Screen"
http://www.ckls.org/~crippel/computerlab/tutorials/mouse/page1.html

Idarose Luntz, Lower School Computer Lab Teacher University School, "Read Any Web Page"
http://shaker.us.edu/useweb.htm

Cal Poly SLO Study Skills Library, "Note Taking Methods"
http://www.sas.calpoly.edu/asc/ssl/notetaking.systems.html

Mind Tools, "Mind Maps: A Powerful Approach to Note Taking"
http://www.mindtools.com/pages/article/newISS_01.htm

FX Palo Alto Lab, "Shared Text Input for Note Taking on Handheld Devices"
http://www.fxpal.com/publications/FXPAL-PR-02-158.pdf

"An Internet Environment for Type-C Note Taking"
http://nr.stic.gov.tw/ejournal/ProceedingD/v12n3/122-128.pdf

Chapman University, "Hints for Good Note Taking"
http://www.chapman.edu/academics/cas/study/noteTaking.asp

Mortimer J. Adler's "How to Mark a Book"
http://radicalacademy.com/adlermarkabook.htm

California Virtual Campus, "Collaborating Online"
http://www.nlight.com/Success/Collab/index.html

California State University Northridge, "Russo's Group Skills"
http://www.csun.edu/~hflrc001/groupsk.html

HCi Services, "Small Group Skills"
http://www.hci.com.au/hcisite2/toolkit/smallgro.htm

Karen Feenstra Iamnext Academics, "Study Skills: Team Work Skills for Group Projects"
http://www.iamnext.com/academics/grouproject.html

Study Guides & Strategies, "Organizing and Working on Group Projects"
http://www.studygs.net/groupprojects.htm

Ivy Tech State College Student Success Tips for the Online Learner
http://www.ivytech.edu/distance/orientation/resources/success/

University of Texas at Austin, Distance Education Center, Submitting Course Assignments
http://www.dec.utexas.edu/onlinecourses/submitassign.html

Capital Community College, "A Statement on Plagiarism"
http://webster.commnet.edu/mla/plagiarism.shtml

University of Alberta, "Guide to Plagiarism and Cyber-Plagiarism"
http://www.library.ualberta.ca/guides/plagiarism/

Purdue University OWL, "Avoiding Plagiarism"
http://owl.english.purdue.edu/handouts/research/r_plagiar.html

University of Wisconsin Writing Center, "Quoting and Paraphrasing Sources"
http://www.wisc.edu/writing/Handbook/QuotingSources.html

Indiana University, "Plagiarism: What It Is and How to Recognize and Avoid It"
http://www.indiana.edu/~wts/pamphlets/plagiarism.shtml

Penn State University Libraries Online Reference Shelf, "Writing Resources/Style Manuals"
http://www.lias.psu.edu/gateway/referenceshelf/writ.htm#cse

Purdue University OWL, "Research and Documenting Sources"
http://owl.english.purdue.edu/handouts/research/index.html

University of Wisconsin's Writing Center, "APA Documentation"
http://www.wisc.edu/writing/Handbook/DocAPA.html

APA Online, "Electronic References"
http://www.apastyle.org/elecref.html

Long Island University, "APA Citation Style"
http://www.liu.edu/cwis/cwp/library/workshop/citapa.htm

Long Island University, "Chicago Manual of Style Citation Guide"
http://www.liu.edu/cwis/cwp/library/workshop/citapa.htm

University of Wisconsin's Writing Center, "CBE Documentation"
http://www.wisc.edu/writing/Handbook/DocCBE.html

University of Washington, "Health Links: AMA Style Guide"
http://healthlinks.washington.edu/hsl/styleguides/ama.html

Ithaca College Library, "Turabian Samples for a Bibliography"
http://www.ithaca.edu/library/course/turabian.html

IEEE Computer Society, "Style Guide"
http://www.computer.org/author/style/

University of Wisconsin's Writing Center, "Twelve Common Errors: An Editing Checklist"
http://www.wisc.edu/writing/Handbook/CommonErrors.html

Purdue University OWL, "Editing and Proofreading Strategies for Revision"
http://owl.english.purdue.edu/handouts/general/gl_edit.html

Purdue University OWL, "Proofreading"
http://owl.english.purdue.edu/handouts/general/gl_proof.html

Purdue University OWL, "Writing Essay Exams"
http://owl.english.purdue.edu/handouts/general/gl_essay.html

Purdue University OWL, "Annotated Bibliographies"
http://owl.english.purdue.edu/handouts/general/gl_annotatedbib.html

University of Wisconsin's Writing Center, "Annotated Bibliographies"
http://www.wisc.edu/writing/Handbook/AnnotatedBibliography.html

University of Minnesota/Crookston, "Writing an Annotated Bibliography"
http://wwlw.crk.umn.edu/library/links/annotate.htm

Cornell Oin Uris Libraries, "How to Prepare an Annotated Bibliography"
http://www.library.cornell.edu/olinuris/ref/research/skill28.htm

East Carolina University Joyner Library Academic Library Services, "How Do I Write an Annotated Bibliography?"
http://www.lib.ecu.edu/Reference/howdoi/annotbib.html

Purdue University OWL, "Research and Documenting Sources"
http://owl.english.purdue.edu/handouts/research/index.html

Capital Community College, "A Guide for Writing Research Papers Based on MLA Documentation"
http://www.ccc.commnet.edu/mla/index.shtml

Weber State University, "Advice from 'Those Who Know' on Taking WSU-Online Courses"
http://wsuonline.weber.edu/studsupport/sucess_stud/advice.htm

Alamo Community College District, "Online Testing"
http://www.accd.edu/sac/history/keller/accdit/SSOtest.htm

Chapter 6: Online Learning Pitfall Solutions

"Benson Relaxation Response"
http://www.oates.org/chris/stress/tip06.htm

Illinois State University, "Personal Workstation Checklist"
http://www.shs.ilstu.edu/hpo/Wellness/WellnessHome/Occupational/
Ergonomics/ErgoLinks/checklist.htm

Roehampton University, "Students' Stress Busters"
http://www.roehampton.ac.uk/stressbusters/computer.asp

Paul Marxhausen, "Computer Related Repetitive Strain Injury"
http://eeshop.unl.edu/rsi.html

San Diego State University, "Online Learning: How to Get the Most Out of Your Online Learning" Experience
http://defcon.sdsu.edu/1/objects/online/

Dayton VA Medical Center, "You Can Do Something About Eyestrain"
http://www.dayton.med.va.gov/pthealth/eyestrain.html

Boston Medical Center, "Eye on computers: Keeping your Focus"
http://www.bu.edu/bridge/archive/1998/12-04/health.html

Larry K. Wan, O.D., "9 Steps to Reducing Computer Eyestrain"
http://www.allaboutvision.com/cvs/irritated.htm

Vision RX, "Computer Vision Syndrome (CVS)"
http://www.visionrx.com/library/enc/enc_cvs.asp

Florida Gulf Coast University, "Technology Skills Orientation"
http://www.fgcu.edu/support/office2000/word/

EducationOnlineforComputers.com, "Education Online for Computer Software"
http://www.educationonlineforcomputers.com/

UC Berkeley Library, "Finding Information on the Internet: A Tutorial"
http://www.lib.berkeley.edu/TeachingLib/Guides/Internet/FindInfo.html

Purdue University OWL, "Searching the World Wide Web"
http://owl.english.purdue.edu/internet/search/

University at Albany Universities Library, "Internet Tutorials"
http://library.albany.edu/internet/

Monash University, "Library Online Tutorials"
http://www.lib.monash.edu.au/vl/www/wwwcon.htm

University of Texas at Austin, "Blackboard Tutorials Student Manual"
http://www.utexas.edu/academic/blackboard/tutorials/student/

East Carolina University, "Blackboard Tutorials"
http://www.ecu.edu/elearning/orientation/Blackboard/Bbtutorial.htm

Regent University, "Blackboard Tutorials" (Video)
http://www.regent.edu/general/student_orientation/tutorials/blackboard.cfm

University of Houston Victoria, "Vista Tutorials"
http://www.uhv.edu/webct/students/orientation/tutorials/vista_tutorial.htm

California State University Chico, "WebCT Tutorial"
http://www.csuchico.edu/stcp/online/tutorial/

WebCT, "Student Tour"
http://www.webct.com/oriented/ViewContent?contentID=1805985&page
Name=student_tour3/intro.html

Muskingum College CAL, "Organization"
http://www.muskingum.edu/~cal/database/general/organization.html

Psychological Skills Press, "Organization"
http://www.psyskills.com/add01.htm

Virginia Tech, "Study Environment Analysis"
http://www.ucc.vt.edu/stdysk/studydis.html

University of Texas at Austin Learning Center, "How to Modify Your Study Environment I"
http://www.utexas.edu/student/utlc/makinggrade/modifystudy
environment.html

Virginia Tech, "Control of the Environment"
http://www.ucc.vt.edu/stdysk/control.html

University of Texas at Austin, "Procrastination Quotient"
http://www.utexas.edu/student/utlc/makinggrade/pquotient.html

University of Nebraska, "Thirteen Timely Tips for More Effective Personal Time Management"
http://www.ianr.unl.edu/pubs/homemgt/nf172.htm

University of Guelph, "Learning Time"
http://www.webshops.uoguelph.ca/learningtime/

Marin Community College, "Managing Time & Setting Priorities"
http://www.marin.cc.ca.us/~don/Study/5time.html

Oregon State University Academic Success Tutorial, "Procrastination"
http://success.oregonstate.edu/study/procrastination.cfm?A=0

TutorNation
http://www.tutornation.com/index1.asp

TutorsDirectory
http://www.tutors-online.co.uk/

Tutors Online
http://www.dctech.com/tutors/index.php

Tutor.com
http://www.tutor.com/

"Netiquette Home Page"
http://www.albion.com/netiquette/

Arlene Rinaldi, "User Guide and Netiquette Index"
http://www.fau.edu/netiquette/net/

Idaho Digital Learning Academy, "Orientation to Online Learning: Netiquette"
http://idla.k12.id.us/Policies/IDLA_Student_Center_Netiquette.htm

"Study Guides and Strategies"
http://www.studygs.net/

Utah State Academic Resource Center, "Online Learning Center"
http://www.usu.edu/arc/index.php?site_id=7

Wilton High School, "Chemistry Coach"
http://www.chemistrycoach.com/lbe4.htm

Chemeketa Community College, "Howtostudy.org"
http://www.howtostudy.org/

Oracle Think Quest, "Learn Physics Today"
http://library.thinkquest.org/10796/ch1/ch1.htm

Dan's Math Lessons, "Math Basic Skills"
http://home.earthlink.net/~djbach/basic.html

Learning Support Centers in Higher Education, "Links to Traditional Learning & Study Strategies Web Pages"
http://www.pvc.maricopa.edu/~lsche/resources/online/ol_traditional.htm

Stress Oasis, "Benson Relaxation Response"
http://www.oates.org/chris/stress/tip06.htm

Anna Purnell, Madison Area Technical College, "Following Directions"
http://www.apurnell.com/images/FOLLOWING%20DIRECTIONS.htm

"How Well Can You Follow Directions"
http://www.justriddlesandmore.com/direct.html

APPENDIX B

Computer Skills Performance Tips

This appendix provides information about key combinations and mouse options that will help you work more efficiently.

Many people have become so used to using the mouse that they automatically go to it whenever they want to perform a menu function or navigate around a document or web page. If they are typing a document in Microsoft Word, for example, and they want to save it, they move their hand from the keyboard to the mouse, click on "File" and then "Save." Or, if they are filling in a form on a web page, they type information into one field and then move their hand from the keyboard to the mouse, click in the next field, and then begin typing again.

Shifting from the keyboard to the mouse and back again only takes a couple of seconds, but over time, this adds up. You can be more efficient by using keystrokes or key combinations. This is not to say that one method is better than another. Use whichever method or combinations of methods you are comfortable with. You will develop your own preferences and use the mouse for some functions and the keyboard for others.

This appendix shows you just a few examples of keyboard shortcut keys and key combinations. Check the application's documentation or do an Internet search on "Shortcut Keys"+(application name) .

Navigation

Some keys and key combinations are used to move from one part of a document or web page to another and even from one application to another (see Table B.1).

TAB	Moves cursor from one field to the next in a form or the next item in a drop-down menu
SHIFT+TAB	Moves cursor to the previous field in a form
ALT+TAB	Switches between open applications
HOME	Moves cursor to the beginning of the line in a document, spreadsheet, etc.
END	Moves cursor to the end of the line in a document, spreadsheet, etc.
CTRL+HOME	Moves cursor to the beginning of a document, spreadsheet, web page, etc.
CRTL+END	Moves cursor to the end of a document, spreadsheet, web page, etc.

TABLE B.1 Navigation Keyboard Shortcuts

Menu Items

There are often two or more different ways to access menu items, or to initiate functions, within computer applications. Most applications allow you to press the ALT key plus the underlined letter in the menu name that appears on the menu bar (see Table B.2).

ALT+f (File)	Opens the File menu
ALT+e (Edit)	Opens the Edit menu
ALT+v (View)	Opens the View menu
ALT+t (Tools)	Opens the Tools menu
ALT+h (Help)	Opens the Help menu

TABLE B.2 ALT Key Combinations to Access Menus

You can often use the CRTL (control) key to go directly to common functions within applications. If there is a CRTL key alternative, it will be listed next to the menu item (see Table B.3).

CTRL+s	Saves the current document, spreadsheet, etc.</TB>
CTRL+a	Selects all of the document, etc.
CTRL+x	Cut
CTRL+c	Copy
CTRL+v	Paste
CTRL+z	Undoes the last command or action
CTRL+y	Repeats the last command or action
CTRL+p	Print

TABLE B.3 CRTL Key Combinations to Access Menu Items or Functions

Some applications use the Function keys, which are labeled F1 through F12 on most Windows-compatible keyboards. But some products make more use of the Functions keys than others. And with the exception of F1 (Help), these keys are rarely used universally for the same function. So consult the application's documentation or Help to find out what the different Function keys do. Table B.4 shows a few of the most common Function key uses.

F1	Opens Help (most applications)
F5	Refresh (Internet Explorer) or Reload (Netscape Navigator)
F7	Initiates the spell checker (most Microsoft applications)
F11	Creates a chart (Microsoft Excel)

TABLE B.4 Some Function Key Uses

Windows Key

Windows keyboards have a "Windows Key" with the Microsoft Windows logo on it. Look for a Windows Key at the lower left and lower right of the keyboard. Pressing this key plus various other keys performs a variety of functions (see Table B.5).

Windows Key	Opens the Start Menu
Windows Key+D	Minimizes all windows and returns the user to the desktop
Windows Key+M	Minimizes all windows
Windows Key+SHIFT+M	Undo minimize all windows
Windows Key+E	Opens Microsoft Explorer
Windows Key+Tab	Cycle through open programs through the taskbar
Windows Key+F	Opens the Microsoft Windows Search window
Windows Key+F1	Opens the Microsoft Windows Help
Windows Key+R	Opens the Run window

TABLE B.5 Some Windows Key Uses

Right Mouse Button

The right mouse button is quite useful in many applications. When you right-click within an application, the resulting pop-up menu provides direct access to some common functions that would normally take several key strokes to accomplish (see Table B.6).

Microsoft Windows Desktop	Arrange Icons, Refresh, New, Properties
Microsoft Word	Cut, Copy, Paste (editing commands), Font, Paragraph, Bullets and Numbering (formatting tools), spelling and grammar tools
Microsoft Excel	Cut, Copy, Paste, Paste Special (editing commands), Format Cells, Insert, Delete, Clear Contents
Internet Explorer	Back, Forward, Select All, Print, Refresh, Properties, Save Picture As, Copy, Add to Favorites
Netscape Navigator	Back, Forward, Reload, Bookmark This Page, Save Image As, View Page Info

TABLE B.6 Some Right-Click Menu Items

APPENDIX C
Glossary

The glossary terms shown here with definitions are provided to help you learn some of the unique language within distance education and to help clarify meanings. The definitions were collected from a variety of sources, including the following websites:

Glossary of Internet Terms

http://www.luminet.net/~jackp/gloss2.htm

Glossary of Terms: Online Education

http://www.ion.illinois.edu/IONresources/onlinelearning/glossary.html

Glossary of Telecommunications Terms

http://www.its.bldrdoc.gov/fs-1037/

There are a number of Internet glossaries where you can look up terms and concepts pertaining to distance education, the Internet, and computer usage.

A

Access provider   A company that provides Internet access, usually for a monthly charge.

Adaptive technology   Technology that has been adapted for use by people with disabilities. A browser with screen-reading technology added is an example of an adaptive technology.

ALN (asynchronous learning network)   A network of people linked for "anytime, anywhere" learning, using the web and other remote learning resources, without the requirement to be online at the same time.

Antivirus program   A program that searches computer files, disks, emails and memory for viruses and then removes or isolates those that it finds.

Applet   A small, non-browser-specific program embedded in a web page that can perform interactive animations, calculations, or other tasks.

Application   A software program that performs a specific function. Some examples are word processors, spreadsheets, web browsers, email readers, and graphics programs.

Assistive technology   A technology used to assist people with disabilities, such as screen magnifier software for visually impaired computer users.

Asterisk   A character (*) used as a wildcard when searching for computer files.

Asynchronous   Communication that does not necessarily occur at the same time. Email and discussion board communication is normally asynchronous.

Attachment   A file, such as a document or image, that is connected to an email message. The recipient must have software that is compatible with the attachment to open it.

B

Back up   To save a copy of a computer file in a location other than the original.

Bandwidth   The amount of data that can be transmitted over a communications channel, usually measured in bits per second.

Bit   Short for binary digit, the smallest unit of data that a computer uses.

Bitmap   A type of graphic image format formed by a pattern of dots or pixels.

Bookmark (Netscape)   A browser feature that allows you to save a reference to a specific website or page.

Bookmarks   A way to quickly locate a website with a web browser. After the site address (URL) is stored as a bookmark, users need not type in the address for access but just click on the bookmark.

bps (bits per second)   The unit of measure to describe the speed of a communications channel.

Broadband   Generally refers to telecommunication in which a wide band of frequencies is available to transmit information. Often used for digital cellular telephones and high-speed Internet access.

Browser   A software program, such as Internet Explorer and Netscape Navigator, used to navigate the Internet and view websites.

Byte   A group of eight bits that represents a piece of data such as a single character.

C

Cache   A temporary storage area used by web browsers to keep data from recently visited websites. This makes downloading the page again faster because the browser does not have to request the data from the website again.

CAI   See Computer-Assisted Instruction.

CD-R (compact disc-recordable)   An optical storage medium for files or programs that a computer can read and can write to one time.

CD-ROM (compact disc-read-only memory)   An optical storage medium for files or programs that a computer can read but not write to.

CD-RW (compact disc-rewriteable)   An optical storage medium for files or programs that a computer can read and can write to numerous times.

Certificate   Credential awarded on completion of a program of courses that does not result in a degree but educates students in a specific area of study. Completion of such a program typically carries with it CEUs (continuing education units).

Certification   A professional credential awarded as the result of passing an examination in a topic, such as computer networking. Someone who obtains certification is considered certified in that topic.

Chat   A form of interactive online communication that enables typed conversations to occur in real time. Your messages are instantaneously relayed to other members in the chat room while other members' messages are instantaneously relayed to you. Often referred to as Live Chat.

Chat room (or chat channel)   A virtual space created by computer software where participants in online electronic education can hold discussions, talking to each other by typing in messages on their computers that appear immediately on each participant's screen. Chat rooms are usually devoted to one particular topic.

Client   A software program (or the computer using the program) used to contact and obtain data from a server program located on another computer.

Collaborative Learning   A learning situation that involves a group working together through technology to delve into content. Students can electronically access other students, the instructor, and resources.

Compressed file   A file in which data is encoded in a way that causes it to take up less space.

Computer-Assisted Instruction (CAI)   Teaching process in which a computer enhances the learning environment by assisting students in gaining mastery over a specific skill.

Computer-based training (CBT)   A training program stored on and accessed from a CD-ROM.

Configuration   Used to describe how a computer or computer software is set up.

Consortia   Entities (singular, consortium) formed by and among schools and other learning providers to meet a specific need outside of the normal practices of any one member.

Contact hour   The unit of measurement used to determine credit granted; one contact hour is equivalent to one hour per week, per term, spent in classroom instruction.

Continuing Education Unit (CEU)   A nationally recognized system of measurement for continuing education programs. One CEU is defined as 10 hours of instruction (contact hours) by qualified instructors in a responsible program.

Cookie   A small file downloaded to your computer when you browse certain web pages. Cookies hold information that can be retrieved by other web pages on the site. Some cookies are programmed with an expiration date so they are automatically disabled after a period of time.

Cornell system   A popular note-taking system.

Correspondence study   Individual or self-guided study by mail from an educational institution. Credit is earned through written assignments and proctored tests.

Courseware   Software consisting of instructional modules that can be used to present lessons. Some examples are Blackboard, eCollege, and WebCT.

Coursework   The assignments, activities, research, exams, or other tasks that are required of students in demonstrating their mastery of the course topic.

CPU (central processing unit)   The unit of a computer where data processing takes place.

Crash   An abrupt, unplanned computer system shutdown caused by a hardware or software malfunction.

Credential equivalency   Recognition of credits taken at one institution as equal to credit from some other institution, especially from one country to another.

Credit   A unit that represents completion of a college course. Colleges usually grant credit in increments ranging from one credit to five credits.

Cross-platform   Software that works on any platform or hardware (e.g., PC or Macintosh). The Internet is cross-platform; proprietary software (like Word-Perfect) is not.

Ctrl (control key)   A key on IBM PC and compatible keyboards that is pressed in combination with another key to produce an alternative function (for example, Ctrl+c will copy highlighted text).

Curriculum   The combination of courses making up a particular area of study. The courses are arranged in a sequence to build on what has gone before.

Cut-and-paste   To cut part of a document or a graphic file and then insert or paste it into another place in the document or into another document or file.

Cyber   A synonym for web or Internet, as used in cybercafe, cyberbuddy, or cyberspace.

D

Database   Any aggregation of data; usually a large collection of data that has been formatted by some defined standard.

Dedicated line   A type of account available from an Internet service provider that connects the customer to the Internet 24 hours a day.

Desktop   In a graphical user interface, an onscreen metaphor of your work, just as if you were looking at a real desktop cluttered with folders full of work to do. The desktop consists of icons that show files, folders, and various documents.

Dial-up account   An agreement with an Internet service provider to connect a customer to the Internet when the modem dials the provider's number.

Digital   Made up of numbers, or digits. On a computer, the digits are binary—only 1s or 0s. Also describes any technology that converts or transmits information signals by breaking them into binary digits.

Digital Drop Box   A location in Blackboard where students send their assignments for instructor viewing.

Digital modem   A modem that communicates computer data directly without having to convert it as an analog modem does; requires an Integrated Services Digital Network (ISDN) line and is faster than an analog modem. It uses a special digital phone.

Diploma   A certificate awarded for the completion of a degree program.

Diploma mill   Term for a scam that promises a degree credential for a payment, with no work necessary.

Discussion   Distance learners may hold a discussion through a chat, bulletin board, group-meeting software, or teleconference; using text messages or voice; and in asynchronous or synchronous mode.

Discussion Board (Bulletin Board System or BBS)   An electronic communication system that allows users to leave messages, review messages, and upload and download software. Also, called a Discussion Forum.

Disk cache   A temporary storage area on a computer to keep data available. For instance, web browser software keeps a certain number of web pages available for revisiting.

Distance education   Teaching or learning by way of telecommunications, or the process of providing instruction when students and instructors are separated by physical distance.

Distance Education and Training Council (DETC)   A national agency in the United States that accredits distance-learning courses and programs.

Distance learning   Learning in which the student and instructor are remote from each other. Distance learning can include one or more of the following media: correspondence courses by mail, audio and videotapes, teleconferencing, videoconferencing, faxing, and use of the Internet to disseminate and exchange information.

Domain name   A unique label for an Internet site.

Domain Name System (DNS)   A database system that translates textual network domain names into numeric Internet addresses.

Download   To transfer a copy of a file from a central source to a peripheral device (such as CD-ROM or DVD) or a computer. You can download a file from a network file server to another computer on the network (for example, from the World Wide Web) or from a discussion board.

Draft Folder   A special folder that contains emails that have been written but not yet sent.

DSL (digital subscriber line)   A type of data communication technology used to deliver and receive information on current telephone lines at a much greater speed than phone service.

E

e   Electronic anything; delivered online.

e-education   Electronic education that uses online media for delivery.

Editor   A computer program used to edit (prepare for processing) text or data.

Educational portal   An educational website considered as an entry point to other websites that commonly include online tools like grade books, real-time chat, discussion boards, online whiteboards, and other course resources.

Elective   Courses that aren't required but which you may take toward the total credit required to obtain a degree.

Electronic Library   A collection of articles or other material that is stored on a library computer for access by online students and instructors.

email   A feature that lets a computer user send a message to someone at another computer using the Internet. Email, or electronic mail, can duplicate most of the features of paper mail, such as storing messages in "in boxes" and "out boxes," message forwarding, providing delivery receipts, and sending multiple copies.

email address   Electronic locator for email delivery: a unique identifying name followed by the @ symbol and then the name of the host organization, which could be a business (.com), organization (.org), university (.edu), governmental entity (.gov), or Internet service provider (.net).

Emoticon   A combination of characters used in email messages, chats, or discussion boards to represent a human emotion or attitude (such as happiness, laughter, sadness).

Encryption   Scrambling of data transmitted via the Internet, to ensure that only the recipient can decode and read it.

Ethernet   A system for linking computers over a local area network (LAN).

Experiential learning   Learning acquired from experiences outside a classroom that may be counted for college credit..

External Link   A URL that takes you to another web page or site.

F

Face to Face (F2F)   Describes traditional classroom instruction.

FAQs (frequently asked questions)   Information files provided by many websites to reduce the need for repetition of information.

Favorite (Microsoft Explorer)   A browser routine that allows you to save a reference to a site or page that you have already visited so you can return to that page at a later time.

Fax (facsimile)   A system used to transmit visual images via standard telephone lines.

File   An organized collection (in or out of sequence) of records related by a common format, data source, or application.

File directory   A way to organize files into a hierarchical structure. The top directory is often called a root directory and is labeled with a letter (such as "C:\" for a computer's hard drive, or "E:\" for a computer CD-ROM drive; these can be set by the user to be alternative letters). Below the root directory are subdirectories of folders and files contained in the root directory (for example, "C:\myfiles\assignmentl.doc" would represent the file "assignmentl.doc" in the "myfiles" folder on a computer's hard drive, or "C:\" root directory).

File format   The format that a program uses to encode data on a disk. Some formats are proprietary, and a file so encoded can only be read by the program that has created the file. Software companies often share formats so that users of one program can save files in the format of another (for example, in Microsoft Word you can save a file in the Corel WordPerfect file format).

File name   The name given to a file so that it can be distinguished from other files. In most operating systems you cannot include the following characters in a file name: " ' \ / [ ] , ? * < >.

Filename Extension   A three-character code at the end of a file name (after a dot) that identifies its type (for example: doc, wpd, wps, rtf, and txt).

Firewall   A system (hardware, software, or both) that is used to prevent unauthorized Internet users from accessing private networks or computers that are connected to the Internet.

Flame   An insulting or derogatory comment included in an Internet discussion, most often in newsgroups. Flames can expand into flame wars.

Folder   In a graphical user interface, an organizing structure that contains multiple files and is analogous to a directory.

Footer   In word processing, printed information (especially title, page number, or date) placed in the bottom margin of a page and repeated on every page or every other page of the document.

Forum   See Discussion Board.

Frames   Web-page layout style in which different content appears in separate areas of the page, allowing an index to remain stationary.

Freeware   Software available for downloading from Internet sites without cost.

FTP (File Transfer Protocol)   A way to move files from a distant computer to a local computer, using a network such as the Internet.

G

Gateway   A computer connecting two systems or networks, translating data to make the information usable by both systems. America Online is a gateway between its users and the Internet, though it is not directly on the Internet.

GIF (Graphics Interchange Format)   A graphics file format used to place photographs and illustrations, animated or still, on Internet web pages.

Gigabit   1 billion bits of data.

Groupware   Software that helps organize the activities of users in a networked group; some groupware allows users to share calendars, plan meetings, and distribute electronic newsletters.

H

Header   In word processing, printed information (especially title, page number, or date) placed in the top margin of a page and repeated on every page or every other page of the document.

Hertz   A unit of frequency used to measure the electromagnetic waves by which sound, light, and energy are transmitted.

Hit   A term describing the numbers of clicks made to access a web page. Not an accurate measure of those who actually use a page, because some browsers must be clicked in several times to call a page up, and there's no indication of how long a user spends at a given page.

Homepage   A web page maintained by a person or organization that contains pointers to other pieces of information.

Host   Computer containing data or programs that another computer can access over a network (such as the World Wide Web).

Hotlist   A list of URLs stored by a browser to allow easy retrieval of a site; similar to a bookmark list.

HTML   See Hypertext Markup Language.

HTTP   See Hypertext Transfer Protocol.

Hybrid course   An educational program that combines various technologies for course delivery and can blend face-to-face and online classes.

Hypertext   A document that has been marked up to allow a user to click on words or pictures within the document to connect to further information.

Hypertext Markup Language (HTML)   A system of codes used to create web pages and access documents over the World Wide Web. Without HTML codes, a document would be unreadable by a web browser.

Hypertext Transfer Protocol (HTTP)   The protocol used to signify an Internet site is a World Wide Web site.

I

Icon   In a graphical user interface, a picture on the screen that represents a specific file, directory, window, or program.

Information Superhighway   Nickname for what is officially known as the National Information Infrastructure (NII), the interconnected global networks of communication and information services, including the Internet.

Interface   A connection between two pieces of hardware or software, or between a user and an application. Also, the appearance of a screen displaying a program—the collection of bars, buttons, colors, and shapes that assist in navigating and operating the program.

Internet   A matrix of networks that interconnects millions of supercomputers, mainframes, workstations, personal computers, laptops, and handheld devices. The networks that make up the Internet all use a standard set of communications protocols, thus allowing computers with distinctive software and hardware to communicate.

Internet discussion groups   Also known as newsgroups, these are collections of individuals who post information and discussions via email on subjects of mutual interest.

Intranet   An internal network for a company, school, or organization that uses the technology of the Internet rather than the complicated software of local area networks (LANs).

IP (Internet Protocol)   The international standard for addressing and shipping data on the Internet.

IP address   A unique identification number consisting of four sets of numbers separated by dots. Every computer on the Internet has an IP address.

IRC (Internet Relay Chat)   A section of the Internet where users can communicate with others by typing messages that appear on the monitors of other users as soon as they are sent. Also, the online group discussion itself; abbreviated as chat.

ISP (Internet Service Provider)   The company that provides connection to the Internet and World Wide Web.

J

JavaScript   A computer language used for the World Wide Web that allows for adding interactivity to web pages.

JPEG (Joint Photographic Experts Group)   A type of graphics format for web pages that provides generally better quality than Graphics Interchange Format (GIF) images but consists of more data and so takes longer to load.

K

Keyword   A word or phrase sought by a search engine. Refers both to the word the user of the search engine types in and to the word listed in an area of the HTML coding for a web page called a metatag. The search-engine software compares the two and provides a list of matches.

Kilobyte   1,000 bytes.

L

Lab fee   A fee paid by a student for access to a computer or other technology facility of a university.

LAN (Local Area Network)   A group of computers that are locally connected on a network.

Learning portal   An organization that provides access to multiple educational providers on its website.

Leased line (dedicated line)   A phone line that is connected 24 hours a day, primarily used for Internet activity.

Link (hotlink)   HTML-coded text or pictures on a web page that, when clicked, allows a view of a different web page on the same site or a different site.

Listserv   An email program or electronic mailing list that allows the distribution of messages to many individuals in one mailing and allows multiple computer users to connect to a single system for communication or discussion. Listserv groups can number in the millions, or may be small groups of people involved in class discussions.

Live chat   Online communication between two or more online persons either by keyboarding or voice. See Chat.

Login   The name of an account used to access a computer system, such as that of an Internet service provider (ISP). Usually used in conjunction with a personal secret password for limited-access sites. Also used as a verb, "to log in."

Lynx   A text-based web browser, easy to read and accessible by older computers because it does not use graphics.

M

Mailing list   A list of users who will receive copies of information on a particular topic that is distributed periodically by email. Mail server software, such as Listserv, receives contributions and distributes them to all subscribers.

Markup   Text or codes added to a document to formulate a document's layout or to create links to other documents or information servers. Hypertext Markup Language (HTML) is a common form of markup.

Megabit   1 million bits of data.

Megabyte   1 million bytes or 1,000 kilobytes. Most commonly used to measure a working memory area of a computer.

Memory   All computer program execution and data processing takes place in memory. Every computer comes with a certain amount of physical memory, usually referred to as main memory or RAM. A computer that has 1 megabyte of memory can hold about 1 million bytes (or characters) of information.

Menu   An onscreen list of available options or commands. The options are usually highlighted by a bar that you can move from one item to another.

Menu bar   A horizontal bar that runs across the top of the screen or the window and holds the names of available menu options.

Mirror site   A File Transfer Protocol (FTP) site that contains an exact copy of the files at another site; developed so that increased numbers of people can access files of popular sites.

Modem   Short for modulator/demodulator. A piece of equipment to allow computers to interact with each other via telephone lines by converting digital signals to analog for transmission along analog lines.

Moderated list   A Usenet newsgroup or mailing list where communications first go to an individual who serves as moderator and approves all items before they are distributed to the group or list.

MPEG (Motion Picture Experts Group)   A protocol for compressing sound and movie files into a format for downloading or streaming over the Internet.

MS Word   A word-processing software developed by Microsoft.

Multimedia   The use of more than one medium in transmitting information; in electronic communication, refers to the use of any combination of text, full-color images and graphics, video, animation, and sound; also, any document that uses multiple forms of communications media, such as text, audio, or video.

N

Netiquette   A set of generally accepted but informal guidelines for considerate conversation and behavior in emails and on the Internet in general.

Netscape   An example of browser software that allows you to design a homepage and to browse links on the World Wide Web.

Network   A series of points connected by communication channels in different locations. Any collective of computers that can communicate and exchange data among themselves.

Newsgroup   A public electronic forum where messages are posted and responded to.

O

Offline   Doing work while not connected to a network.

Online   Actively using a computer, especially one connected to the web. Using a computer network to complete course requirements.

Online course   An educational program whose primary delivery source is the Internet. Communication is asynchronous, occurring through email, listservs, multi-user object-oriented environments (MOOs), threaded discussions, and chat rooms.

Online service   A company that maintains a network of information, forums, and other services, including Internet access, and charges a fee for participation. Among the major online services are America Online, CompuServe, and the Microsoft Network.

Operating system   A computer program used to provide basic services like files, screen information, and mouse use. Microsoft Windows and Apple MacOS are the most common operating systems for personal computers.

P

Pass/fail   The grading system for a course that offers no specific letter or number grade, but only the option of failing or passing the course based on a single level of acceptable performance. Pass/fail courses result in credit, but they are recorded as P/F on a student's transcript.

Password   A series of letters and/or numbers used in conjunction with a user name to provide security while accessing a site or joining a class.

PDA (Personal Digital Assistant)   A lightweight, handheld computer, often featuring software applications that provide calendars, calculators, address books, and other useful resources. New models commonly have an internal modem and cellular phone to be used as a link to a larger computer or the World Wide Web.

Pdf   A document designation used by Adobe's Acrobat software. Allows documents to be stored and downloaded, maintaining graphics and typesetting.

PIN (personal identification number) or PID (process identifier)   A personal identifier used as part of security on entering sites.

Plug-in   A software program that works with another software program to add more functionality to it.

POP (Post Office Protocol)   An older protocol that enables an email program to retrieve messages from a server.

Pop-up menu   A menu that appears on the screen in response to a user action (such as a right-click on the mouse) and is separate from the primary application menus.

Post   The term used for placing a message in an online communications area called a bulletin board or discussion group.

PowerPoint   Software that creates a visual presentation or slide show.

Proctor   Someone who oversees students taking tests.

Proctored exam   An exam setting where a student is monitored while taking the test. In distance learning, some organizations set up remote proctored exam scenarios to accommodate distance learners.

Protocol   A formal set of standards, rules, formats, or systems that assures uniformity between computers and applications, as for exchanging data.

Pull-down menu   A pop-up menu that appears directly beneath the item selected on a menu bar.

R

RAM (random access memory)   Allows a computer to keep information stored for instantaneous access, as opposed to retrieving it from a hard drive, which takes more time. Information in RAM is lost when you turn off the computer or lose power.

Real-time chat (Internet relay chat or IRC)   A network of Internet servers through which individual users can hold real-time online conversations. Instant messaging is a type of real-time chat.

Regional accrediting agency   One of several regional agencies in the United States that sets standards for educational quality and coordinates those standards with other regional agencies for consistency among schools.

Rich Text Format (rtf)   A file format with special characteristics like lines, boxes, and special fonts.

Router   A relay that connects a local area network with other networks.

S

Screen-reader software   Any software product that converts text into spoken language to assist visually impaired computer users.

Search engine   A website that hosts an indexed database of many of the websites in the world, to make searching them possible. The search engine is programmed to match words the user types in. Google, Yahoo!, and Excite are well-known search engines.

Server   A computer that provides information to client machines. Web servers send out web pages, mail servers deliver email, etc.

Shareware   Software that may be tried for free, then bought for a small payment if the user keeps the program.

Shortcut   In Microsoft Windows, a file that allows quick access to another file (such as a software application, word-processing document, or Web page).

Signature   A short text message that can be automatically included at the end of each email and that contains contact information (such as name, address, phone number, email address, etc.).

Snail mail   Nickname for regular paper mail from the U.S. Postal Service.

Software   The programs, programming languages, and data that control the functioning of a computer's hardware and direct its operations.

Spam   Unwanted commercial email, mass-mailed like paper junk mail. Can be filtered out.

Streaming audio   Web technology that allows you to hear audio files as they are downloading, reducing waiting time.

Surf   To browse through information presented on the Internet by casually following links you think might lead to something of interest.

Surfing   As in "surfing the web"; to move from one website to another.

Syllabus   Information given to the students enrolled in a course, such as objectives, textbooks, expectations, grading policies, contact information, and an outline of all the lectures, exams, and assignments that make up the course.

Synchronous   Taking place at the same time (such as real-time chats or instant messaging).

T

Telecommunication   The science of information transport using wire, radio, optical, or electromagnetic channels to transmit and receive signals for voice or data communications using electrical means.

Test of English as a Foreign Language (TOEFL)   A standardized test of competency in English that some colleges require for foreign-student applications.

Thread   A series of messages on a certain topic that have been posted on a discussion board, typically using visual indicators to illustrate which messages are replies to which other messages. Often referred to as "threaded discussion."

Transcript   Official record of the courses a student has taken at an educational institution.

Transfer   The process by which a student moves from one learning institution to another. The rate at which information moves between a sender and receiver.

TCP (Transmission Control Protocol)   A protocol that makes sure that packets of data are shipped and received in the intended order.

Trojan horse   An insidious and usually illegal computer program that masquerades as a program that is useful, fun, or otherwise desirable for users to download to their system. Once the program is downloaded, it performs a destructive act.

24/7   Twenty-four hours a day, seven days a week. Used to describe the hours of operation of online courses or how often technical support is available for online students and teachers.

U

URL (Universal Resource Locator)   The address of a homepage on the World Wide Web.

Upload   To copy a file to a website where others can access and read or download it.

Username   The name that you use to access your online course or login at a website. Often written as "userid."

V

Virtual university   Higher education institution that does not have a physical brick-and-mortar presence but uses technology to connect educators and learners.

Virus   An insidious piece of computer code written to damage systems. Viruses can be hidden in executable program files posted online.

W

Web browser   See Browser.

Web portal   A website considered an entry point to other websites.

Web server   A computer on which server software has been installed and that is connected to the Internet, allowing the computer to accept requests for information using the HTTP protocol.

Web-based training (WBT)   Training materials stored on a website that a student accesses and uses online.

Web page   A file on the World Wide Web that is accessible using a web browser.

Website   A set of interconnected web pages, usually including a homepage, generally located on the same server, and prepared and maintained as a collection of information by a person, group, or organization.

Whiteboard   A feature of online meeting software that enables participants in remote locations to draw or write on a virtual "board" and have this work visible to all participants.

Wide Area Network (WAN)   A network composed of Internet connections.

Window   A rectangular portion of a display screen set aside for a specific purpose.

Wizards   An automated instructional guide that is a feature of some Microsoft and other software applications. Wizards can provide application shortcuts for accomplishing specific tasks.

Word processing   Using a computer to create, edit, and print documents such as letters, papers, and manuscripts.

Word processor   A computer-based typing and text-editing system.

Worm   An insidious and usually illegal computer program that is designed to replicate itself over a network for the purpose of causing harm or destruction. Whereas a virus is designed to invade a single computer's hard drive, a worm is designed to invade a network.

WWW (World Wide Web)   A graphical hypertext Internet navigational tool allowing access to sites, files, and homepages created by individuals, businesses, and other organizations. Also called the web.

Z

Zip   To compress the data in a file so the file is smaller and therefore takes less time to send over the Internet.

Index